BOTH SIDES OF THE FENCE

DAVID CORBETT

BOTH SIDES OF THE FENCE

A LIFE UNDERCOVER

MAINSTREAM
PUBLISHING

EDINBURGH AND LONDON

To preserve his own safety the author has adopted a pseudonym.

First published in Great Britain in 2002 by
MAINSTREAM PUBLISHING COMPANY (EDINBURGH) LTD
7 Albany Street
Edinburgh EH1 3UG

ISBN 1 84018 769 7

This edition 2003
Reprinted 2004

A catalogue record for this book is available from the British Library

Typeset in Badhouse and Van Djick
Printed and bound in Great Britain by
Cox & Wyman Ltd, Reading, Berkshire

ACKNOWLEDGEMENTS

BIG HUG TO my best pal, friend, lover and wife. Ditto.

To Claire and Gillian – the best girls in the world. Very proud of you both. Love you tons.

Thanks to Dani Garavelli of *Scotland on Sunday* for having faith in my story and helping me to pull it together.

Mum and Dad – thanks for giving me the chance all those years ago to make a life.

Ian, Margaret, Gordon and Linda – thanks for listening and understanding when times were hard.

Special thanks to close friends for being loyal when questions were being asked of you: Big Craig, Pauline, Jim, Marie, Paul and Karen.

Not forgetting the LPD. Just keeping you guys in the 'loop'.

To Strathclyde Police – thanks to all the good guys that I've worked with over the years. You know who you all are, we've shared the laughs. Be safe.

Finally to the good people of Blyth. Keep up the fight.

CONTENTS

1

LIVING ON BOTH SIDES OF THE FENCE

LOOKING BACK, I can see I was always walking a tightrope between respectability and a life of crime. Throughout my adolescence, my future could have been decided by a toss of the coin – cop or robber, goodie or baddie. Either path would have brought me the adrenaline rush I sought like a junkie desperate for his next fix.

Although my father was a police officer, my closest school friends were the sons and daughters of Glasgow gangsters. Caught between two cultures, I lived a double life, quickly learning to fit in wherever I found myself.

To my family I was, by and large, a well-spoken and obedient teenager, who dressed smartly and obeyed the rules. But at night, far from my parents' gaze, I flirted with crime. For several years, I ran with a crowd, stealing cars and fighting with rival gangs in the city's notorious nightclubs. That my only contact with Barlinnie, Scotland's largest prison, has been as a detective, is due largely to my father's determination to better himself and his family.

His desire for a middle-class lifestyle often placed him close to the brink of financial ruin. But it meant that where most of the Gorbals boys faced a life of deprivation, I was given a choice. As they began to filter off into borstals and other institutions, I left them behind to follow in my father's footsteps.

The lessons I had gleaned from them, however, were vital for my future and helped me reach the pinnacle of my profession. As I taught myself to act, speak and even think like one of the gang, I was honing skills that would be critical in a career where one word out of place can betray your identity and end your life.

I was born in 1958 in a one-bedroom flat in a tenement in Crown Street in the Gorbals, Glasgow, an area teeming with large immigrant Irish Catholic families. It was more than a decade before the bulldozers moved in and tore down the sandstone buildings and replaced them with the high-rise flats which were to destroy any sense of community and which have now themselves been torn down. But the razor gangs that gave Glasgow its 'No Mean City' tag were already rife and regular 'slashings' were meted out by the Cumbie – the Gorbals' main contenders.

My father, who at that stage trod the beat in the city centre, would have been entitled to a police house. But he was a proud man who saw no reason to be beholden to the force. In those days, corporation houses were in short supply, so we ended up in a factor's house on the top floor. By today's standards it was tiny: a bedroom with a kitchenette in one corner. But, as there were just the three of us to share it, and we had the luxury of an inside toilet, we were considered lucky. Our neighbours all shared a communal toilet in the backcourt with newspaper for toilet roll. It was a standing joke amongst the children of the close that if you wanted to find out what was happening in the world, you just had to ask one of them to bend over and read their arses.

I lived in the Gorbals until I was six and I always remember it as cold and muggy, your breath visible in front of you as you walked. In those days the trams trundled down Crown Street and sometimes they would bring home my father from a late shift, with his cape draped over his shoulders, ready for a stiff whisky. As soon as he stepped over the threshold, he would blow his nose hard into a handkerchief. It would be black with the soot he had inhaled and he would mutter under his breath about the pollution.

One night, when sugar was in short supply, he came home by tram with two black-market sugar bags, supplied for favours rendered, hidden in his back pocket. But as he jumped off the tram, he slipped and, unbeknown to him, ripped his trousers. All the way home, the children followed him along the street as though he was the Pied Piper, catching the sugar as it fell. By the time he reached the house, there was only a handful left.

In those early days, my parents did their best to cocoon me from the increasing violence on the streets and in friends' homes. But when I was tucked up in my bed, the Cumbie would be out fighting the Toryglen Toi, a gang from the other side of the city. Every so often a friend's father would appear with his face slashed after a street battle and my parents would explain this as an accident at work. But in the backcourts, where the children played, jumping from dyke to dyke (the roofs over the common bin areas), there were always older brothers who knew the truth. They would regale us with stories of the night's skirmishes, embellishing them no doubt for their captive young audience.

As they re-enacted the 'slashings' dished out by their elders, we would beat the dustbin lids and chant Cumbie war cries. As children in more prosperous parts of the city played Cowboys and Indians, we played gangs. It was part of our heritage and we took it for granted.

My father never discussed his job in front of me and it was never a big deal amongst the other children, although they knew what he did and teased me about it. In those days, police officers still commanded respect and a clip round the ear for troublemakers would not end in a lawsuit.

Even so, my father could see the tide was changing and by the time I started primary school, he was looking for a way to get us out of the area. Earning just £5 a week, he was always going to struggle, so he sold his most treasured possessions – a motorbike and sidecar and his cine-cameras and projectors – to fund our move upmarket and across the River Clyde to Scotstoun.

The first time I set eyes on our new house, in Duncan Avenue, I couldn't believe all that space could be meant just for us. Dubbed a 'Victorian cottage' by the estate agents, it seemed positively palatial. Instead of a close, there was a front door and a hallway leading to not one, but three bedrooms. Downstairs we now had a room known as a lounge for visitors in addition to a living room and a kitchenette. And instead of a backcourt, there was a garden with a fence round it.

The culture shock could not have been greater. Where children in the Gorbals had snotty noses and wore hand-me-downs, knitted pullovers and the same shirt five days a week, Scotstoun pupils had proper uniforms with blazers and ties. After school, we would play in Subutteo clubs and football teams with their own strip. Awestruck, I remember asking my parents: 'Are we going to stay here forever?'

At this time everything was going well for us. My father's career was taking off; he had moved into the Land-Rover section of the police and was earning a higher salary. We owned a car and we now spent our holidays in the south of England.

My father was one of seven children, the only one who owned his own house, and I remember my grandfather puffing on his pipe and saying proudly: 'Your dad has made it. He's a toff now.' As for me, I had many happy times in my new home, although even here I sometimes felt the odd one out. Scotstoun was a predominantly Protestant area and, although my father was Church of Scotland, my mother was Catholic. I had been brought up in her faith and, along with just one other boy in the street, I attended the Catholic school, St Paul's Primary.

My reservations were not religious. At that age I couldn't have cared less about my friends' theological beliefs, but I did resent the better choice of extra-curricular activities their school offered.

While Catholic schools focused on religious education and offered us the chance to be altar boys, my neighbours would go off to the Boys' Brigade meetings and camp. It seemed to me that they had much more fun.

As I grew older, I realised that most of our neighbours, who were buyers and sales reps and teachers, were slightly wealthier than my family. Whenever there were parties in the square, we would be allowed to stay over at each other's houses and I would notice, with just a touch of envy, that they had more clothes and toys than I did.

My father, with his more modest salary, could not compete. He was already living beyond his means trying to provide the best for his family.

Gradually the car disappeared, the holidays stopped and, from time to time, shadowy figures turned up on the doorstep.

By this time my father's younger brother Dunc had moved in with us. A police cadet, he was earning next to nothing. Just seven years my senior, Dunc left home because, after his father's death, his mother, my gran, began to regard him increasingly as a financial burden and a hindrance to her bingo playing. One day Dunc, my father and I went out to buy a hi-fi, but when we brought it home, there was an almighty row. My mother was outraged and would not allow the record player to be used in her presence. When visitors remarked on it they were met with a frosty reception. This hostility went on for months and now I understand: she was angry because the money spent on the hi-fi could have been used to better ends.

Although money was always tight, my parents clung on to the house in Scotstoun until I was about to start secondary school, when they finally realised they would have to move to a smaller property. They managed to buy a house in leafy King's Park, one of the most salubrious areas of Glasgow's Southside. Our new home would have fitted into our Victorian cottage three times over, but its location made it more socially acceptable and brought my parents out of the doldrums. On the way to King's Park, they took me past my Gorbals close and said: 'Look how far you've come.'

Despite the dangers I have encountered throughout my life, the yard of Holyrood Secondary, at that time the largest school in Glasgow, was one of the most daunting places I have ever been. Although the school's catchment area encompassed up-market King's Park, the majority of the pupils were from deprived areas such as the Gorbals. They were tough and streetwise and scared of nothing.

On the first day, I was dropped at the gates and watched in terror as hordes of screaming children seemed to bear down on me. I immediately understood that in my pristine uniform, with my straight tie and my shining shoes, I was going to stick out like a sore thumb. I was small for my age even then and everyone seemed to tower above me in the chaos of the playground. I felt I would be trapped forever in that swirling cauldron of activity. But, eventually, teachers began to arrive and impose some order by dividing us into the classes that were to dictate our destinies over the next few years.

Because we had sat the 11-plus exams, we were all immediately streamed according to our perceived abilities, which was bad news for me. I had never excelled academically and it was inevitable that I would end up somewhere near the bottom. In fact I found myself in 1E, the second-lowest class, full of people seen as too stupid to educate. All that was missing from most of my new companions was a bolt in the neck. Their noses ran all the time, their fingernails were filthy and they all had a distinctive body odour. I was the only one in the class with a blazer and I looked like Little Lord Fauntleroy.

I was a soft target and for a few weeks my life was a nightmare as I became the butt of all their schoolboy jokes. But I quickly learned my lesson. Like a chameleon, I learned to adapt to my surroundings, to fade into the background and eventually to become one of the crowd. The minute I waved goodbye to my parents in the morning, I ditched my blazer and dropped my accent until I was indistinguishable from the others in my class. I stopped making my way into the dining hall for lunch and opted instead for a bag of chips and a packet of cigarettes on a street corner, becoming a clone of those around me. Gradually, it emerged that many of the boys were old playmates from my days in Crown Street. We swapped stories about our pasts and gradually I became accepted, even liked.

From the beginning, however, school was a pointless exercise. Everyone in my class was stereotyped as a loser and seen as unworthy of the resources invested in more intelligent children. If 1A's maths teacher was off sick our teacher would be transferred so the clever pupils didn't lose out; we would be left to our own devices. For our part, we did our utmost to live down to our reputations, skipping school as often as possible and congregating in fields behind the local police station.

In Scotstoun, the most daring escapade my friends and I had got up to was to climb over the wall of an old stable and make it our own private den. But I was now in a different world, one of families who viewed crime as a trade, the skills of which were handed down from generation to generation.

While I went home at night to the safety of my house, some of my classmates were helping their older brothers break into the backs of lorries for a share of the spoils. It was second nature to them. I remember them coming in to school with a tale of how the local butcher's shop had been burgled and laughing because everyone in their street had tucked into a Sunday roast.

As these children grew older they went out to steal alcohol, smashing the windows of off-licences and grabbing all they could carry. Now and again, a large crowd would go into a shop and while the leaders threatened the shop assistants, the others would be emptying the premises of its stock. It wasn't long before I was getting involved in their illegal activities. My father, who had moved into the mounted section of the police, spent a lot of time away at horse shows, while my mother, who had begun a job in a factory, was working long hours. Their absence gave me the opportunity to taste the seedier side of life.

Although crime was a fresh enterprise for me, I was a willing and adept student. Indeed, my competitive nature meant that I worked very hard to ensure I was as effective in my new career as my counterparts – and even less likely to be caught. I found that I was increasingly getting a buzz from the street fights and stealing, becoming hooked on the criminal excursions.

At the weekends, we used to get dressed up in the latest fashions – the Levi stay-press trousers, the cowboy shirts and the Oxblood Dr. Martens boots with the yellow laces – and go into the city centre to 'cause some damage'. Armed with knives and razors, we would seek out rival gangs at our favourite haunt, a tacky nightclub called 'Zhivago's'. Although I never slashed anyone myself, I stood next to my friends as they did. The gangs from Easterhouse were much wilder than we were. They carried machetes inside their jackets and some of the people I hung around with never recovered the use of their fingers after their tendons were severed during drunken skirmishes.

Another craze taking off then was joyriding, although we didn't use that word for it. One day one of the boys from our school turned up in a Ford Escort. At first, he wouldn't tell us where he had got it, but after we had been for a spin, he told us it was stolen. After that we all started taking them. In those days it was so easy. Cars weren't alarmed and you could start one by sticking a screwdriver in the ignition. And there was no computer database. When someone reported a car missing, it was registered in a logbook that the police officers were supposed to check at the beginning of their shift. So the only way you were likely to be caught was if a beat officer stumbled across you in the act of breaking in. Most people in the Gorbals wouldn't report you; they were more likely to be leaning out of their windows having a laugh. But even if they wanted to report you, they had no phones so they would have to run down to a police box, by which time the car doors would be wide open and you would have disappeared into the night.

Of course, the engines in cars were not as powerful then, but there was a street renowned as a venue for racing, emergency stops and handbrake turns. More often, however, we would use them to go on day trips, to Balloch on Loch Lomond, or to Ayr on the West Coast, and enjoy a taste of freedom.

The only time I was caught was on one of the countless occasions when I stole my father's car from his own garage. By this time Dunc was a police officer based in Govan. He spotted me behind the wheel and told my father and I got a leathering, but in general I got away with my nocturnal forays, as I wasn't bringing trouble to the door. Dunc realised I was hanging out with the wrong crowd, but it was difficult for him to say anything. Although he took me aside and warned me from time to time, he did not tell my father, who might have taken it as an implied criticism of his own judgment. Anyway, soon after Dunc moved to a neighbouring estate and the heat was taken off me.

Another shameful episode revolved around my short-lived attempt to set up a pop band with some friends. The band was called 'The Nazz' and I was to be the drummer after my father lent me the money to buy a state-of-the-art drum kit. I was supposed to pay him back when we started to get gigs, but, as we failed to be recognised as Glasgow's next big thing, he only ever got one instalment. In order to raise further funds, we stole a violin from the music room at Holyrood Academy. We tried to sell it at The Barras —

Glasgow's outdoor market – but we were told it was too obviously illicit. Eventually a second-hand music shop took it off our hands for next to nothing, even though the shopkeeper must also have known it was dodgy. It was a long time ago, but I still feel guilty about having stolen something that was supposed to help us learn to play music, even though we failed to make much of a profit out of it.

We had some fun in the band's short lifetime. Tony, the singer – who went on to become a proficient car thief, stealing any model to order – had a strong voice and was good-looking, so the girls adored him. We liked hanging around Tony because we always hoped we could go out with the girls he didn't want. But my heart wasn't really in music and, truth being told, I lacked the rhythm to make it work. We got a few afternoon gigs in a cinema, but we never made it on the pub circuit and we didn't stay together very long.

Despite the fact that I was so heavily involved in the gangs, there was another, more tranquil side to my life I was equally comfortable with. Every night, I would go back to my father and mother, where I would behave like the perfect son. It wasn't that I was acting out a part in either place, it was just that, like Jekyll and Hyde, there were two entirely different, and equally valid, sides to my personality that I needed to express. And so I fitted in wherever I went. If I visited my classmates' homes in the Gorbals, I was able to banter with their mothers saying: 'How is it going? I hear the old yin was drunk again last night.' But I also knew what was expected of me in my own home and how to impress my father's police officer friends with my politeness.

At home I would listen, genuinely interested, as the officers talked about their work, my ears pricked for any operational intelligence my alter ego could use to evade capture. Mostly, my father's anecdotes focused on his bizarre experiences. My favourite tale – which I would ask to hear time and time again – concerned his early days in the police, when he was on the beat in the Gallowgate, an area of the city heaving with pubs. One night, he and a colleague were asked to clear one of those pubs after a customer appeared to have died while enjoying a quiet pint on the premises. The man was still sitting upright in a stall, his drink within grasp. On checking, my father and his colleague confirmed the landlord's suspicions. The man, who was stiff as a board, had no pulse. Despite this, the officers were required to wait for the arrival of the surgeon to pronounce life extinct and, so as not to waste valuable drinking time, they left the corpse where it sat and went through to the bar for a dram. Suddenly they heard strange noises from the stall and rushed through only to find the man had vanished and the side door was lying wide open. At first they thought they had made a mistake with their diagnosis. But when, terrified, they ran out, they saw two figures heaving the corpse along between them, like Burke and Hare, as the corpse's feet dragged along the ground. Thinking the man was simply drunk and that the police officers were waiting for the van to take him to the police station, they had decided to mount a rescue operation. A lengthy chase ensued, but eventually the men gave up running and dropped the body on the ground, where it sustained a severe injury to the forehead. My father's short career flashed before his eyes. How were they going to explain the gash on the corpse's forehead to the doctor? Perhaps he would think it was murder and an inquiry would be mounted. When the doctor turned up, however, they came clean. Laughing, the doctor dug into his bag and brought out a sticking plaster, which he placed over the gash, before writing 'Damaged in Transit' across it.

Drinking was part of the police culture in those days, even on duty, where a dram in every pub was considered one of the perks of the job. It was also the way in which police officers let off steam after a stressful day and there were always several bottles of whisky in our house. On Saturdays, when as a member of the horse section my father would often find himself on duty at football matches, he used to get changed and go to the pub for a couple of drinks with his friends before heading home. On one occasion, however, I arrived home to find him still in his uniform, sitting in the living room, his face void of expression. It was the day of the disaster at Glasgow Rangers' Ibrox stadium where 65 football fans were crushed to death, when, as the match was nearing its end, a stairway collapsed and the supporters were trampled underfoot. My father had been on duty outside the ground and was called in, but by the time he got there the bodies were all laid out on the pitch. He said he had never seen anything like it in his life and suffered flashbacks for a long time afterwards.

My father was a good, honest police officer, who knew when the wool was being pulled over his eyes. But there's a level of policing above that, occupied by officers who know exactly how far they can bend the rules to get results, and he was too straightforward to excel at that. Although he spent some time in plain clothes, he quickly became disillusioned with the attitude of a colleague who, he believed, was tipping off criminals when their houses were about to be raided. This shocked my father, but I suspect the reason the officer was doing what he was doing was not that he was receiving backhanders, but that the suspect was giving him detailed intelligence which, the officer believed, would eventually lead to more significant arrests.

The nurturing of snouts, informants or grasses was something only detectives were encouraged to do and, in later years, my father would also be sceptical of the creative approach I took to getting results.

He really only came into his own when he joined the mounted section. A truly great horseman, he travelled across the country demonstrating his skills and became the first mounted police drummer in the country – an incredible feat that involved steering the horse with his feet while using his hands to beat out the rhythm.

Even in the horse section, however, he was held back by forces beyond his control. Because he had married a Catholic, he was blackballed by the masons, a formidable force in the police service even today. Back then, it was common practice for members to hold meetings at which officers up for promotion would be coached for both the interview and examination and my father was barred from attending. The bigotry didn't make him bitter, though, and throughout my adolescence he tried to persuade me to become a police cadet. I was riveted by his stories but, at that stage, I never considered following in his footsteps as peer-group pressure was persuading me to look in other directions for my thrills.

I did, however, have three friends with a degree of ambition and they were to be my saving grace. My greatest aptitude was for swimming and I used to go to a club once a week, where I met Des, Andy and Charlie. They started off in 1D, the class above me, so I was initially a bit of an outsider, but we grew much closer as we got older. They had an entirely different attitude to life and were interested in their futures.

As we turned 15, my classmates were beginning to find their way into borstals and young offenders' institutions. But Des, Andy and Charlie spent hours talking about their careers: Andy wanted to be a trainee draughtsman, Charlie wanted to be a panel beater and Des hoped for a career in the police. One of them would ask: 'What about you, Dave? What do you fancy doing?' There would then be a silence because all I wanted to do was mess around in the gangs.

In the end, I walked away from school halfway through the year with O Levels in English and Technical Studies. The teachers reckoned I was wasting my time. I loved cars and thought I would like to try my hand as a mechanic. One of our neighbours helped find me a position as an apprentice and I was enthusiastic at the prospect of learning a trade I would enjoy. But within ten days, it was clear my dream was not going to be realised. I was allergic to engine oil and my skin flared up whenever I touched it. As a result, my first career was over almost before it had begun. I was devastated. At a loss as to what I should do next I went along to the careers office at Langside College in Glasgow where they suggested I became a trainee sheriff's officer. Amenable as always, I decided to give it a try.

It was with some trepidation, however, that I went along to an interview in a creaky old office in the city centre. I remember my stomach churning as I went through wood-panelled corridors and up a long, winding staircase. I was interviewed by an awe-inspiring old man – about 6 ft 3 in., with white hair, glasses and an artificial leg. I was terrified, but I played the game. I told him I lived in King's Park and that my father was a police officer; the man assumed I was a respectable lad and I left his office with a job. At that time, I had no idea what a sheriff's officer was or what I would be doing. But as I progressed from office junior to second witness to the serving of warrants and to poundings (selling off of property to obtain money on behalf of the pursuer) I realised I had become the shadowy figure that used to appear at my parents' Scotstoun home. I was learning new skills – how to use a typewriter and to communicate – but I was also going into the poorest areas of the city and forcing families who were struggling to survive to pay their creditors. Most families could just about afford to put food on the table. I stuck it for two years, but I always knew I would leave eventually.

If it hadn't been for my job as a sheriff's officer, however, I would never have got a taste of the rush police work could bring. One day, I was out with the sheriff officer when the car behind us somersaulted off the road and down a 50 ft embankment. We were the only people on the road to see it go down so we stopped and ran to help. When we reached the scene, the car was still spinning and the engine was running. There was a couple trapped inside the wreckage and they were obviously holidaymakers as their luggage was strewn everywhere. Between us we managed to turn the engine off, pull the couple clear and administer limited first aid. I just got this incredible buzz, similar to the buzz of running with the gang, but this time I had done nothing wrong. Soon the police, ambulance and fire engines turned up and we had to give a statement and go, but I was on an incredible high for the rest of the day. The following morning I was on the bus going into the city centre when I saw that the guy next to me was reading the *Daily Record* newspaper. There, on the front page, was a picture of myself and Jack at the scene, with the caption: 'Roadside Heroes'. A freelance photographer had taken the picture from the top of the embankment and made us famous for 15 minutes. Des, Andy and Charlie were very impressed by my sudden notoriety and I dined out on the saga for a fortnight.

The accident marked a turning point for me because it came at a time when I realised I was walking a razor's edge. On one side was the adrenaline rush of stealing cars and on the other was the less risky, but frankly tedious, prospect of respectability. It wasn't until I saw the car turn upside down that I realised I could have it both ways. I could live a constantly exciting life, without breaking the law. Less than a fortnight later I was watching *Z Cars* on television with my girlfriend, Lindsey – whom I met at school and who would become my wife – when I realised I was getting a thrill just from watching fictional police officers at work.

The next thing I knew we were on a bus, heading for the police station to pick up a Strathclyde Police application form. I didn't tell my father then, but later, when a letter arrived calling me up for interview, I broke the news. He had almost given up hope of his only son going down the path he had trodden, but now his dream was being realised. His pride alone told me I had done the right thing.

2

THE ROOKIE DAYS

AFTER THE INITIAL euphoria died down, I realised joining the police was not going to be as easy as it sounded. At 5 ft 7.5 in. I was half an inch short of the minimum height restriction and, even with my strong police background, the force was not prepared to overlook this. Instead, after measuring me several times, the officers in charge of recruitment told me to go away and come back in six months when, as a growing lad, they hoped I might have gained enough height to meet their strict requirements. In the meantime, my father taught me how to stand up as straight as a rod, with my shoulders thrust out and up, to make the most of the little height I had. On my return, I was nervous, especially when I saw the other candidates, most of whom were more than 6 ft. But, with four pairs of thick socks on, and my heels as far off the ground as I could raise them without being caught, I scraped through, and was allowed to join the cadets. Although my diminutive stature provoked dozens of nicknames throughout my career, it was rarely to prove a disadvantage when out in the field. Indeed, it meant I could be used as a runner in tense situations, and it made me less conspicuous when, as an undercover, I lived amongst drugs dealers and gangsters. No one would ever suspect such a short man of being a police officer.

Compared to the difficult years that lay ahead, life in the cadets was one big adventure, with lots of sporting activities to keep us fit and weekends away from home. There was an easy camaraderie amongst this crowd of high-spirited adolescents, all of us desperate to make it as regular police officers. We came from many different backgrounds – boys from the Gorbals mixed with doctors' sons from Bearsden, a leafy suburb just outside the city. But we all had something in common: our desire to join the police service. We were hungry to get on the beat and start making arrests. But equally we were typical teenagers, willing to take advantage of any opportunity for bad behaviour our trips away from home afforded us.

For six months, the cadets were given a taste of all kinds of police work, via secondments to different divisions and to specialist departments, such as traffic and the dog section. Some of the younger boys were treated as gofers and were forced to carry out menial tasks, such as sweeping out the cells. But, as I was a bit older and everyone knew my father and uncle were police officers, I was given better jobs like travelling in the van when prisoners were being taken from the station to the court.

Outside of work, I also had more responsibilities than most of my fellow cadets because, although I was only 18, I became a father soon after I joined up. Although neither of our families was particularly religious, Lindsey and I had been very nervous about telling them she was pregnant. But they were both very supportive and said they would stand by us whatever we decided to do. In the end, we got married and, a few months later, Lindsey gave birth to our first daughter, Claire. For a while we moved in with my parents who were by now living in East Kilbride, a new town, around 15 miles from Glasgow and then, because of the overcrowding, we qualified for a council flat in the town and soon had a place of our own. We had no money because a cadet's wage was pitiful, but Lindsey came from a big family and everyone mucked in to give us old pieces of furniture. For the first six months, we had no car so I was commuting into Glasgow every day by bus. Yet, despite all this, we had no regrets and I was happy both domestically and professionally. I was particularly lucky because my swimming abilities were quickly identified and I was picked out for Strathclyde Police cadets' five-strong life-saving team, which competed in pools throughout the country. The exercises were often nerve-racking. The team would be called into the pool and handed a slip of paper telling it to enact a particular scenario. I was the captain and had to direct the operation. Eventually, we made it to the British finals in Cheshire, but, to the horror of our instructors, we threw it away at the last hurdle – the temptation to spend the night before the competition drinking was just too much for us.

Left to our own devices in the police headquarters where we were staying, we bought a carry-out of Tartan Special and began horsing around. By 11.30 p.m., we realised we had better get to our beds, so we bundled all the empty cans into a black bin liner which we hid in my room. But, as the banter died down and sleep beckoned, I decided I had to get rid of the evidence of our drinking session. I opened the door of the room next to mine and hurled the black bag in there. Everything went quiet again, until the cadet in the next room took the same decision and opened the door next to him. This went on for some time, until the last member of the team ended up with the bag. Half asleep, he staggered out of his room and slung it into the next one, where the superintendent in charge of us, an ex-Army officer with waxed-back hair, was entertaining some of his friends. The morning after the night before, we came a poor fifth, but the laugh we had was worth the telling off we got from the trainers.

Another highlight was the week I spent with three other cadets at the mounted branch with my father and his colleagues, most of whom I knew. Because of the family connection, we were all treated like part of the team, which was a novelty for us. The week finished with a horse show, in which the cadets were used to help demonstrate the skills of the horsemen. At the end of the day, the horsebox got stuck in the mud and we were called in to lift it out. We got filthy, but when we got back to the stables, we were given fresh shirts and trousers and told to shower, before being whisked away to a pub where we were fêted by the older officers. A lot of the Mounties had won rosettes and the atmosphere was tremendous. We all drank Glayva (whisky liqueur) from a huge silver cup and then the Chief Inspector announced there was to be an award for the cadet of the day. I won it and the others were laughing and saying it was a fix because my father worked there. But it was all good-natured and I was happy to be the centre of attention. It was a long time before I was to be as happy again.

It was December when I joined the regulars. I remember the Christmas lights blinking as a group of breathless cadets made their way across the city to take their old uniforms with the blue-band hats back to the clothing store in Albion Street to swap them for the real thing. We must have presented a strange picture, high as kites, but self-conscious, with our short haircuts and our black polythene bags containing our cadet uniforms slung over our shoulders as we walked over the suspension bridge to the dusty office, one of our instructors leading the way. Inside, an old man who smelled of smoke opened the shutters to the lift. You could tell he had seen it all before and was thinking: 'Look at this shower of smart-arses.' All thoughts of how foolish we looked, however, vanished when we were handed our new uniforms. Just seeing the chequered hat brought a lump to the back of my throat. I couldn't wait to get home and try it on. And, later, there we all were in my parents' house, Lindsey sitting with Claire on her knee and my father sitting on the floor saying: 'This goes with this. That goes with that,' and my mother making sure the creases in my trousers were in the right place. Little did I realise at that moment, with my hopes so high, that the following year would test my endurance to its limits.

Two weeks later, after an induction course, I was posted to Cranstonhill police office, one of the busiest in the force, to begin my new career. If you wanted the bright lights and the buzz, then Cranstonhill was the place to work because it covered the city centre, where all the drinking and fighting went on. It was divided into five sections, each with their own characteristics and each demanding different skills. In the red-light area – Blythswood Square and the surrounding streets – a sharp operator would learn how to use the prostitutes as informers; in Woodlands, a predominantly Asian area, you would need to be a good communicator, sensitive to ethnic tensions. But the most sought-after section was Sauchiehall Street, the busiest part of the city, where restaurants, pubs and dance halls all jostled for space and the gangs fought to prove their supremacy. I soon learned I was to start my probation in the red-light district and I was raring to get to work.

My father had always been emphatic about first impressions and I had taken his lesson to heart. He used to say that if your boots were clean, you'd shaved and you had a smart haircut, then you could be as thick as two short planks but the public would respect you. 'You could be talking Arabic, but the public will think, "That's a smart officer" and they will put their faith in you,' he said.

I took his lesson to heart and was determined not to come across as a daft wee boy. Indeed, so eager was I to prove my professionalism that, before starting my first nightshift, I went on a reconnaissance mission to find out the best place to park my father's car. I had butterflies in my stomach when I left the house at 10 p.m., but I was confident I looked the part. Unlike some other probationers, I knew better than to take my sandwiches wrapped up in a polythene bag, and I went in with my raincoat folded, exactly the way my father had showed me.

But all my efforts did nothing to make me feel less intimidated or to improve the reception I got when I arrived. I walked through the back door and it was like walking onto the set of *Hill Street Blues*. As the shift was changing, there were shirts going on and coming off and I had to cut my way through the smell of smoke and stale alcohol. At first I thought: 'God, the prisoners are stinking.' But then I realised the smell was coming from the police officers.

From there, I walked into a long, narrow room with a row of lockers at one end and school-style desks at the other. In front of the desks was the lectern at which the Sergeant stood to give out his instructions at the start of the shift. His papers were already in place. My mouth was dry and I was already thinking: 'I'm out of my depth. I've done the wrong thing here.' One or two young men who were obviously probationers were already in the room, but they barely acknowledged my existence, save for a grunt in my general direction. I took a seat right at the back and began to stare desperately at the clock, the hands of which appeared to be nailed in place.

After what seemed like hours, the doors swung open and an awesome figure strode through them. He was wearing his raincoat, with his newspaper folded under his arm, his pockets bulging and his torch sticking out the top. His hand was on his hip and his hat was to the side and he bellowed over to me, 'What the fuck are you sitting there for?' The other probationers all turned round to stare at me and I meekly got up and moved along one. Inside, I was panic-stricken. I was thinking, 'This is really bad. I'm starting off on the wrong foot.'

The door opened again and another officer with sallow skin walked through and said: 'Oh, God, Jimmy, we've got another one. Move son, that's my seat.'

By this time my ears were burning red, but the penny had dropped – all the older officers must sit at the back. I shuffled forward. One of the old timers said a phrase I was to hear constantly over the next few years, 'TJF'. I later found out from my father this meant 'The job's fucked', a favourite saying of the old cops. To cover my embarrassment, I started writing feverishly in my notebook, but that just made me look more ridiculous because nobody had said anything.

Other officers were entering the room in dribs and drabs now and I heard someone say: 'Who's the unlucky one that's going to get lumbered with him then?' Finally the Sergeant began to read out the numbers which told you which beat you were on, but it all sounded like gobbledygook to me. '455 on 34/35 beat; 452 on 47/48 beat.' Once you understood the system, it told you what you were doing that night. I wrote all the numbers down, then scrabbled round trying to find the officer that I was on with, but nobody told me anything. Someone handed me a radio, but didn't show me how to use it, so I put it in my pocket the wrong way round and everybody laughed. And then someone was shouting: 'You're with him,' and I turned round to see a man with silver hair and a massive potbelly. My 'mentor', Ian, would not have looked out of place in a monk's habit and he was to teach me the hard way the first lesson all probationers learned in those days: you are the lowest of the low. Your only function was to be the butt of the older officers' ill humour. A probationer had no allies. The probationers above you, even if they only had a few months' service, were so glad to have moved up the pecking order that they kicked you even harder than the older officers. During the first terrible months I spent in Strathclyde Police, I made a pledge that I have always kept, that never in my life would I ever treat anyone of any colour or creed the way I was treated at Cranstonhill.

The main reason the older officers hated to be lumbered with a probationer was that they had their beats sewn up. They knew where they could get a drink or a cup of coffee at any hour of the night or day and they spent their shifts moving from pub to pub, getting free drinks at every hostelry. It was an accepted part of the culture those days, like lifting a packet of fags at a break-in, or clearing a pub just so you could enjoy a lock-in with the publican. It was as if they had marked their territory and the new boys were intruders. They didn't know if they could trust you to keep quiet and they weren't willing to take the risk.

Every night for the first few weeks, the routine was the same. Ian would say to me: 'You're going to sit in the police box on the corner of West Campbell Street and read the log book tonight and then I'll come back for you and you won't tell anybody what I've done.' And sure enough, when we got to the corner, he put me inside the box and shut the door. I couldn't believe it. Here I was, a married man with a daughter, going out to work to keep my family, and I was being shoved in a box. It was so humiliating. I would wait in the freezing cold for an hour and a half before Ian returned, smelling of whisky, and then we would walk the streets, without exchanging a word, until the Sergeant came and took me back to the police office for my break. I would go back out for the second half of the shift and the whole farce would be repeated.

It didn't help either that I failed an early trust test. On one rare occasion, I was allowed to stop for a drink with Ian. The following day another officer asked me where I had been, and, stupidly, I told him. The word spread quickly: 'The boy can't keep his mouth shut.' But things reached their lowest ebb when an officer, who had seemed to be amongst the easiest to get on with, asked me what my religion was. When I told him I was Catholic he went straight back and shared the information with the rest of the shift. As a result, the abuse got worse and every night it would be: 'Who's getting the pape tonight?' ('pape' is Glasgow slang for a Catholic and/or the Pope). If I had been an accepted part of the team, I might have thought the jibes were meant in good humour, but I was the outsider and it was clearly intended as abuse.

In those early days, I would go home every night and say to my father: 'This is not what I joined the police for.'

He would just smile enigmatically and say: 'Go with the flow. It will get better and you will learn the trade.'

And eventually Ian did start opening up a little bit. He told me how he dealt with 'neds' – slang in Scotland for the troublemakers we encountered every night on our rounds. 'If you see them hanging around a street corner, never move on to the road to pass them, wait for them to move and let you past,' he said. 'It shows the public the respect you command. If they won't move, then arrest them at a later date for something else and say: "That's for not moving off the corner".'

The methods the officers used then were harsh and would not be considered acceptable today, but they did work. One day, Ian walked up to a bunch of old winos drinking out of bottles and lined them all up against a wall. He turned to the first one and barked: 'I've told you McGuire, I don't want to see you on my beat again. The next time it's jail for you.'

McGuire replied, 'Right, sir,' and walked away.

Ian did the same to two others, but the fourth was a bit of a hard case, ready for a confrontation. 'What's that you're drinking?' Ian asked him.

'My usual tipple: hair tonic,' came the reply.

Ian took the bottle from him, opened the tramp's trousers and poured it down the front of them. 'What do you say?' Ian demanded.

'Thank you very much, sir,' the tramp answered.

Another night, Ian and I were walking in the red-light district when a prostitute started swearing at him. He told me to walk on, while he sorted it out. Later on, I saw the woman lying on the ground with a bloodied nose. Ian just said: 'It's all right. She'll move on now.'

There were also good things about the way the system worked then. Because officers took pride in their own beats, they would notice if a blocked drain hadn't been fixed and would take it on themselves to pursue the council. On the down side, however, I began to realise that some of the officers I was with were not so very different from the toerags in the Gorbals I thought I had escaped.

Yet, despite my apprehension, I stuck at it and soon found myself at the Scottish Police Training College in Tulliallan, near Kincardine, where for eight weeks I was forced to live a life totally alien to me: a regimented, studious life, where everyone was in bed by 11 p.m. and up again early in the morning. It was not a routine I liked, but I was desperate to earn my spurs as a police officer and I managed to pass the exams and go back to Cranstonhill with a little bit more confidence than I had before.

As a result of the course, I was allowed to use my own initiative more often and it was not long before my enthusiasm, and my nose for the job, paid off. My first arrest was a notorious house and shop breaker, who had evaded capture for quite some time.

I had been out in eight section, in the West End, where hard-drinking pubs stood next to Orange halls. It was about 3 a.m. and the other officers had taken a few beers and had decided to go into Yorkhill Hospital, where they could sit and play cards in the canteen with their radios switched on. I, however, had to walk back to the Cranstonhill office for my tea. I was on my own, walking towards the city centre, when I saw a man gesturing to me from the window of a flat and pointing to a nearby shop. Still a bit naive, it took me a second to understand what he was trying to say, but then I realised: 'He's pointing out that there's something dodgy going on.'

The adrenaline was already rushing through my system because I was alone, but I reached for my torch and headed in the direction he had showed me. I could feel the blood surging through my veins, but I didn't want to call for help and look stupid if it turned out to be nothing.

When I got to the shop, however, the grille was off. There were strange noises coming from inside and I instinctively knew that, so long as I did not mess up, I had an opportunity to make a name for myself. I was terrified, but I was sure the man in the window was still looking at me to see what I would do next. I wanted to prove I was capable. I shone the torch into the building and saw a dimly lit figure in the background. I lifted the radio. Although I had never called for urgent assistance before, the words came out clearly and without hesitation. I could hear my voice in the distance as if the words were being uttered by someone else, and the reply came quickly. 'Alpha Mike Two attending from Yorkhill Hospital.' It was amazing. All these officers who didn't really like me, who saw me as an upstart, a 'pape' and a 'short-arse', would still come to help me because I was a police officer in need of back-up. I could feel the buttons pop off my shirt with pride and, suddenly invincible, I decided to tackle the man myself. I went in and, in the half dark, I could see the infamous James Moor brandishing a knife at the top of the stairs.

Moor had been pointed out to me on many occasions in the past, usually with the caveat, 'You'll never catch him', so I knew what a big fish he was and I felt like Hercules. I said to myself, 'I'm going to have you,' and I went at him with my baton drawn. The blade went down and I grabbed the front of his shirt and swung him round as if in a schoolyard brawl. By the time assistance came, he was cuffed and ready to be taken away.

At first, my colleagues appeared to be amazed and full of plaudits. They said, 'Ya beauty, wee man,' because Moor hadn't been jailed for a very long time and here he was caught in the act. A conviction was a certainty. But then, the next thing I knew, my 'body' had been taken away from me. He was thrown in a police van and there were five guys around me changing the story and writing the case up for me. In the end they took all the credit, with my name mentioned only in passing. On top of that, I came in for more abuse because I was perceived to be a cheeky wee upstart who had shown up the older officers by getting a very good result.

I realised then that police work was a game and the competitive streak in me meant I had to learn to play it better than anyone else. In those days other officers were little more than booze-bags. They could teach me the paperwork but I had more raw talent than them. I had an affinity to lowlife that meant I instinctively knew when people were up to no good. I was determined to exploit my greatest asset and to show my colleagues how effective real policing could be.

3

BEING ACCEPTED

IRONICALLY, IT WAS luck, not the expertise I had gained, that led to me finally winning acceptance among my colleagues.

One night, I was tramping the beat along Sauchiehall Street with Dougie, the officer who had barked at me most aggressively on my first day in the job. A veteran of Cranstonhill, he commanded the loyalty of all the other officers, although it was given more from fear than from respect. As usual, Dougie looked a mess, his newspaper sticking out of his pocket, his hands behind his back and his hat to one side. Yet, in front of us, the crowds of revellers parted like the Red Sea to let us pass.

Up ahead, we could see trouble had broken out at a notoriously rowdy pub called the Maggie. Vast quantities of alcohol had been consumed at a stag party, a furious argument had broken out and the fighting had spilled out onto the street. Dougie, who was well used to such carnage, walked into the fracas without a second's hesitation but as he grabbed one of the drinkers all hell broke loose. Customers started swarming out of the pub to attack us. There were bottles and fists flying everywhere, and, before I knew it, I was being spun round by one of the stag party. I managed to radio for assistance, but the next time I looked for Dougie, I saw he had been floored. There was blood coming out of his mouth, but there was nothing I could do to help him as by now assorted furniture was being hurled in my direction.

Then, suddenly, from out of the Glasgow smog, there appeared a succession of black cabs. Like extras in a western, the drivers jumped from their seats and headed purposefully towards us. At first I thought that they too had come to have a go at us, but instead they marched into the midst of the saloon-room brawl and started clearing the place. I could see them, as if in slow motion, lifting troublemakers by their arms and legs and hurling them this direction and that across the room. Minutes later, with hardly a man left standing, the cavalry disappeared into the night.

By the time the other police officers turned up, I was on my feet, although my tunic was ripped and my hat was over the other side of the road. I was standing with my baton out, surrounded by bodies, their limbs poking in different directions. It must have been a pretty impressive sight because the section Sergeant was dumbstruck. Finally he spurted out: 'For God's sake, Dave, what have you done?' followed by, 'Don't worry. We'll sort this out.' It was the first time he had called me by my Christian name and I could detect a sneaking admiration in his voice.

Dougie had a broken jaw and was taken to hospital, but when he came to, he couldn't have been more grateful. 'I wouldn't like to fall out with you. You must have felled seven or eight of them,' he said. With this ringing endorsement, my reputation was secured. I had saved the shift legend, and, if old Dougie decided I was one of the lads, then no one was going to argue with him.

Naturally, I didn't tell any of my colleagues about the mysterious army of taxi drivers who had saved our skins. Instead, I built on the myth that had inadvertently been created by explaining that, at the time of the incident, I had a lucky baton given to me by my father. As a result, I threw off my 'cheeky wee upstart' image and earned my first nickname: 'Dinky', which, as always, played on my height. It was a term of endearment that stayed with me for more than seven years.

The Maggie showdown was a Godsend in that it opened up career opportunities that would not normally have come my way so early in my career. In particular, I was allowed to spend some time in plain clothes where my talent for undercover work, born of my misspent youth with Gorbals gangsters, was immediately apparent. Sent on a mission to catch thieves that had been breaking into cars in parts of the city centre, I used my knowledge of the way criminals operate to devise a new strategy that paid dividends.

Other officers had tried and failed to catch the culprits red-handed but I reckoned I knew the reason why. The other officers had all been using the Glasgow School of Art as a lookout point because it was central to the area in which the thieves were operating. But, by the time they had spotted the offence taking place, run down the stairs and out the front door, the criminals were long gone. I thought about my own short time as a car thief and, together with an enthusiastic young officer – who is now an inspector – came up with an alternative plan.

All along the art school were 20-ft-deep 'dunnies', or basements, with pipes running the length of them, more or less at street level. It was possible to climb over the railings and drop onto these pipes so you were only a few feet from the parked cars, yet practically invisible to passers-by. We did this for five late shifts and we made arrests almost every night. As soon as the thieves had their fingers on the car radios, we put the handcuffs on them. The whole operation tested our bottle, but the buzz we got each time the tactic worked was unbelievable. And, of course, the kudos didn't go amiss either. At the end of the week, the Chief Inspector came out and praised us in front of the shift and, at that moment, I knew that, if I was given the chance, deep undercover work would be the making of me.

From then on, whenever there were spare men on the shift, I was asked to go out in plain clothes. I gained confidence and started speaking back to the older officers who had given me such a hard time at the beginning. However, they continued to moan, 'The job's fucked.' I learned over the years that they were complaining about the wages, rookies, bosses and everything else to do with their job. Rather than say what was wrong it was easier to say 'TJF'. Sometimes I used to say to old Dougie, 'Tell me if you need to be turned over. I don't want you to get bedsores from sitting on your fat arse.' He would laugh and hurl back some insult. As a result, the other probationers, who had been too scared to stand up to these guys, began to see there was more to the job than sitting in pubs all night complaining, 'The job's fucked.' They were keen to become more involved on the frontline. You could feel the tide was turning away from the old and sometimes corrupt practices in favour of more proactive policing, but it was going to be a very slow process.

In the meantime, salaries were low and it was difficult not to get sucked in to the culture of drinking and of helping yourself to what were almost universally considered the 'perks' of the job. Once you were accepted as part of the team, you would have a lot of laughs and accumulate a wealth of anecdotes with which to entertain your friends. But you would also put on weight and begin to stagnate professionally, until you could see that, 20 years down the line, you wouldn't be so different from the older officers you had initially despised.

Drinking on duty was actively encouraged as a way to gain intelligence. But at times, it led me into scrapes, which were hilarious, but would be severely frowned upon today. Most embarrassing was the saga of 'Winkie', when a notorious housebreaker slipped through my fingers in front of a busload of gawking passengers. Winkie was a friend of James Moor, but while Moor was in jail, he had continued plying his trade in the community. Mostly, Winkie was breaking into offices and, although he wasn't getting away with a lot of money, he was doing a lot of damage to the properties.

One Sunday late-shift, when I had spent several hours drinking with another colleague, called Jimmy, a message came over the radio that an alarm had been set off in a nearby office block. Simultaneously, Jimmy and I stopped supping and said, 'That'll be Winkie.' We knew we were close enough to catch him if he was heading for home. We were busy debating his route when who should come flying round the corner but Winkie himself.

At this point, our night took on the air of an episode from the *Keystone Cops*. Winkie was running so fast that he didn't see us start to chase him, but we had drunk so much our legs were like jelly and we kind of staggered along behind him, puffing and sweating as we went. As we ran along Argyle Street, one of the city's main arteries, it seemed as if we might lose him, so, although we were reeking of alcohol, we jumped on a Number 64 bus and shouted: 'Follow that man.' We jumped off as he approached his tenement flat and pursued him up the close. There was nowhere he could go, so we were sure we had got him trapped. But when we got to the top of the stairs it became clear he was not going to come without a fight. He moved towards us aggressively and Jimmy grabbed his hair. As he did that, I raised my baton and swung it, but it missed him and Jimmy took the full blow. Jimmy shouted out in pain and let go of Winkie.

As I bent down to assess the damage, Winkie ran back out of the close – much to the amusement of the passengers on the bus, which, unbeknown to us, had stopped at the end of the street to watch all the excitement. When Jimmy and I emerged clutching each other, a sarcastic round of applause greeted us before the bus moved on. As a result, we had to return shame-faced to Cranstonhill where we told our bosses Jimmy had fallen chasing the nameless suspect through the back closes.

Such excesses were not unusual, although it was unusual for them to have such bizarre consequences. One nightshift we sat drinking in the Park Bar, off Argyle Street, from 1.30 a.m. to 5.30 a.m. As dawn broke, we fetched the newspapers from the shop next door and gave them to everyone in the pub. After we had read them, we bundled them up and put them back. If you were given the job of policing the Modern Homes Exhibition in the Kelvin Hall it was great, because the alcohol was free flowing. You would be drinking from the time you came on at 2 p.m. until 11 p.m. It was accepted practice and nobody would ever have made a complaint against you.

Although I never got myself involved in anything illegal, my lowly rank meant I was sometimes forced to turn a blind eye to the outrageous behaviour of other officers, despite disapproving of their activities. In fact, through no fault of my own, I once carried stolen property in the back of my car. I had offered an older officer a lift after a particularly gruelling nightshift, and, on our way out of the station, he said to me: 'I've got a job to do on the road home.' Immediately, alarm bells started ringing and I thought, 'What's he getting me into?' But, as his junior, there was very little I could do about it. He asked me to park the car and then disappeared, only to come back clutching a polythene bag, which he put in the boot. It turned out that on his beat the officer had caught someone breaking into a car and chased him away. When he returned, he discovered a toolbox lying on the road, so he took it and hid it. Then he fetched the owner and asked him what was missing. The owner told him he could not see anything. It was either the thief's toolbox or the car owner was too tired at having been woken up at such an hour to have noticed.

It was strange. This officer was a family man, who would never have considered breaking into someone's car or home. But he didn't consider taking the toolbox to be stealing, any more than people working in offices consider taking envelopes and stamps to be theft.

I couldn't get him out of my car quickly enough but I would never have reported him to my superiors, because, for all I knew, some of them might be involved in such activities themselves and it would have been the easiest way to kiss goodbye to my career. Such behaviour was not uncommon. When a radio message went out to say a pub had been broken into, the patrol cars used to race each other to the premises. They knew that whoever got there first could pick up a freebie and mark it down as part of the thieves' haul.

There were some senior and hugely unpopular officers who were prepared to stand up for what they believed. One superintendent used to turn up at burglaries and pat the sides of officers' raincoats to see if they had anything in their pockets. I was never going to be the Serpico of the Police Force, rooting out corruption as the famous US officer did in New York, but I did feel uneasy and disillusioned with the way some of the things were going in my rookie days. Now, 25 years on, Strathclyde Police is one of the most professional forces in the UK, if not in Europe.

On a good day, I loved the camaraderie and the thrill of catching criminals. But I hated the pitiful pay packet at the end of the week and the way in which I was allowing whisky and junk food to curb my aspirations. In fact, conditions were so bad that I did leave the service for a short time, to take up a more lucrative job driving for an electrical chain store. Like my father before me, I was living beyond my means. I was behind in the payments for my car and my second daughter, Gillian, was on the way, so the extra cash was welcome. I rose rapidly through the ranks, becoming an assistant manager of one of the branches within the year. But I was bored and, as soon as I had cleared my debts, I asked for my job in the force back. I returned to the same shift, where nothing had changed, except that the salary was slightly better. The lads kept asking: 'Has Dinky been hiding in his locker for a year?'

To them it was as if I had never been away. But I had matured and proved that I could make something of myself and I had got used to earning more money. In order to make that kind of money in the police service, you had to turn yourself into a commodity. My father always said, 'Use the police force as a prostitute. Screw everything you can out of her.' I wasn't promotion orientated but I did want to try my hand at everything and so I followed his advice. I went to every section and on every course I was offered, including a driving course, which allowed me to become divisional driver for a while, picking up senior officers on a Friday night and chauffeuring them around.

In plain clothes and during a spell on the vice squad, I learned to use prostitutes as sources of intelligence and as informers. If any offices were broken into in the red-light district, I would pick one of the girls out and say, 'I'm looking for a turn on this. If you help me I will put the word round that you're not to be arrested this weekend, but I need a result.' And then, more often than not, the prostitutes would come up with a name and earn themselves a free weekend. At the same time, I absorbed as much as I could about their lifestyle, an exercise I was to repeat many times as an undercover. I tried to get inside their heads and to speak their language, to understand why they walked the streets and who pimped for them. The prostitutes taught me about giro-drops, where people use false addresses to claim benefits they are not entitled to, so when it came to investigating them, I understood how the system worked and I knew where to go for information.

The effort I invested came in useful again later in my career. Several years later, the relationship I had built up with the prostitutes meant I was drafted in to help investigate when one of them, Linda Carroll, was strangled in a multi-storey car park in the city centre. The 24-year-old woman was pregnant and had planned to give up street walking. It was always going to be difficult to find her killer as no witnesses had come forward but officers were drafted in to monitor the registration number of all the cars using the car park in the weeks after the murder. One of those was a Vauxhall Cavalier belonging to Alexander Galbraith, an outwardly respectable, married man who worked for an offshore oil company in Aberdeen.

At first, he denied having been anywhere near the car park on the night of the murder. But forensic experts discovered fingerprints on a car-park ticket that matched Galbraith's. He was questioned for three days before he broke down and confessed to having killed her.

Eventually he was jailed for four years after he was cleared of murder but found guilty of culpable homicide. Although it was a tragic case, it was rewarding to know we had caught the man responsible and that a jury had convicted him.

In years to come, when I found myself at the centre of the investigation into the murder of Arthur Thompson junior – the son of Glasgow's Godfather – there was to be no such satisfactory conclusion.

4

THE SHOP WINDOW OF THE FORCE

I ENJOYED MY remaining years at Cranstonhill, but eventually I decided there was nothing to gain from staying on the beat in the city centre. I applied for and was accepted by the Support Unit, otherwise known as 'the Untouchables', 'the Hit Squad' or 'the Special Patrol Group'. At this time it was said that the unit was in the shop window of Strathclyde Police, meaning all eyes were on us due to numerous high-profile jobs.

The unit was made up of 10 teams of around 25 officers, who were parachuted in to tackle particular crises. If there were a riot or a sudden upsurge of a particular crime, such as burglary, in one division, the white vans with their distinctive orange stripes would be brought in to sort it out. The Support Unit was also responsible for conducting search and seals in advance of VIP visits and, eventually, for providing firearms expertise when necessary. Its duties were so wide ranging that it was an excellent opportunity for officers who wanted to broaden their skills.

The weekend before I joined the Support Unit I was given a traditional sending off by the boys at Cranstonhill. My leaving do was at the Polish Club, one of the shift's favourite haunts. A few days earlier, there had been an amateur dramatics night and there were still props scattered everywhere in the basement. We had been telling jokes for hours when I left the room to use the toilet and I could hear howls of laughter emanating from the bar.

I feared the worst: I was going to be stripped naked and tied to a lamppost or some such other prank. But when I returned I found a coffin had been placed in the middle of the table and I was expected to spend the rest of the party in it. That was to be my swansong from the division on what was one of the funniest nights of my life.

I quickly came down to earth, however, when I discovered that I was not being sent to Springburn – the estate in which the city branch of the Support Unit was based – as I had expected. Instead it had been decided that I should be sent out to Motherwell, in Lanarkshire. This did not appeal to me at all, as I liked to be in the thick of things, although I understood that it was not personal but policy. Strathclyde Police had only come into existence in 1975, shortly after local government reorganisation had created Strathclyde Regional Council. It was a super force created by merging several smaller ones. And, as always with such amalgamations, the city slickers thought they were superior and dominated the scene. In order to bridge the cultural gap, the management decided to send the streetwise Glasgow boys out to the sticks to pass on their expertise to the country bumpkins – or at least that's how they saw it. I stuck it out in Motherwell for six months but I didn't like it. It seemed to me that Lanarkshire criminals were of a different breed, harder even than their Glasgow counterparts. Many of them were from former mining families, who were used to clinging on by their fingertips as the pits closed down and they were forced to survive on the breadline. By then, even Ravenscraig, the steelworks that gave Motherwell its employment, was hanging on by a thread. It was a deprived town, a hard town and the neds had been given the run of it. Working there, in an alien community, made me so depressed that at my six-month assessment I asked to be transferred to Springburn. But it wasn't until my father had a quiet word with one of his friends, a chief inspector, that my request was granted and things began to pick up.

The great thing about the Support Unit was it gave you carte blanche to dive straight into the fracas, to get your hands dirty and start making arrests. If estates such as Easterhouse didn't have enough officers to deal with a gang fight and it was getting out of hand, force control would call for one of the teams from the Support Unit and they would go straight there. If there were bottles or other missiles being thrown, the team might decide to send a runner in ahead; the unit would fire someone into the midst of the skirmish to make an arrest, and, because I was eight inches shorter than everyone else, it was always me. It was very physical work, so you had to be very fit. To make sure we were always at our peak, we would have to train twice a week, with three-mile runs and five-a-side football, which suited me down to the ground. Ironically I never heard 'TJF' said once in the unit.

It was less our strength, however, and more our patience that was required when we were sent to keep order over the pickets during the Miners' Strike of 1984–5. Where in England the most violent scenes were between the striking miners and the scabs – those who defied the ballot and kept on working – in Scotland the industrial action at the collieries was more solid. The worst confrontations took place at Hunterston ore and coal terminal in Ayrshire and at the threatened Ravenscraig steelworks in Motherwell as coal was picked up from the former and transported 50 miles to the latter in a convoy of Yule and Dodds lorries. It was our job to ensure the lorries' safe passage. The pickets were extremely well organised, with their own buses and good intelligence, and they would race from one to another, causing as much disruption as possible.

We would park our van down a side street outside Ravenscraig and watch the miners as they ate their sandwiches and read their newspapers, and for a while everything would be good-natured. Then we would get word that the lorries, sometimes as many as 60 of them, were on the motorway. We would start marching up towards the picket line in twos and the miners would realise the coal was on its way. At first there would be some banter and joking, but as the lorries drew nearer, we switched into our role as police officers and they switched into their role as miners. It became them against us, and there would be shoving and spitting and needles stuck into us. The miners would even push cigarette ends into the backsides of the police horses in order to make them bolt and throw the mounted officers off. We would end up shouting and kicking back until the lorries were finally through. And then it would start all over again. Sometimes, we would get a call from our colleagues at Hunterston saying they needed assistance and we would blue-light it all the way to Ayrshire. Or we would be told about an opencast mine selling coal and we would have to try to beat the flying pickets there. It was a crazy situation and it went on for months and months. As the miners did without their wages, we were raking it in on overtime. We were making so much money you would hear officers talking about the 'miners' suite' they had bought for their living room or their 'miners' car'. Towards the end, when the pit workers were weary and facing defeat, and we were fed up with policing picket lines all day every day, the atmosphere began to get very tense. The miners took out their frustrations on the only people available, the officers on the frontline, and it wasn't long before we were rising to the bait. As they laid into us, we would wind them up, shouting, 'We made lots of money this week thanks to you. How much did you make?' It was wrong, but we were tired of being the fall guys, of being pawns in a political battle that didn't really involve us.

Of course, crowd control was only part of our function. Soon after I transferred to Springburn, I was sent on the training course of a lifetime to learn how to conduct search and seals. Run by the Army at RAF Burtonwood, in Cheshire, it worked on the premise that those on it were under permanent threat of attack. From the day you arrived, until the day you left, there were traps set for you – as we quickly found out to our cost. Even after hours in the bar or in the privacy of the bathroom, you were not allowed to relax.

We had only just arrived when we were sent to a huge bin shed and told, 'There's been an explosion here. Now you have to search the rubble for evidence.' While we were in there, the door opened and an army sergeant, determined to catch the Glasgow team out, threw in a thunder flash. None of us had ever experienced anything like it. Our ears were ringing, our eyes streaming and we couldn't see anything, but it taught us an important lesson and for the rest of the training course we were constantly on our guard. We were shown how to check for paint fragments around light switches and shower cords in case they had been tampered with and how to use a cane to test the floor. If one of the tiles had been lifted, it would sound different and it would be uneven.

You were taught that if you were entering a building at night, you should carry a piece of string held out in front of you and to keep your eye on the base. If there was nylon gutting laid across the door for trip explosives, then the base of the string would bend, and you would call for help. Despite all the tricks of the trade, however, it was made clear to us that if terrorists were good enough at their job, then there would be little a search and seal could do to prevent them. A digital bomb underneath the floorboards that was not intercepted by officers caused the explosion at the Tory Party Conference in Brighton in 1984, killing five people, including the MP for Enfield Southgate, Eric Taylor, and Roberta Wakeham, the wife of the then Chief Whip, John Wakeham. As the IRA said at the time: 'We only have to be lucky once. You have to be lucky every time.'

Several days later, the Glasgow team got its own back on the Sergeant who threw the thunder flash into the bin shed. We handcuffed him, threw him into the back of our van, took off his shoes and took him for a drive down a runway. At the far end, we kicked him out and let him walk back. But despite that, he had the last laugh. We were just about to drive away in our van at the end of the course when he shouted, 'Goodbye,' and threw a thunder flash into the vehicle. These things were strong enough to blow the windows out, so we all dived for cover, screaming and trying to get out. But he had taken the fuse out of it and it did not go off.

Equipped with this knowledge, I took part in many search and seals, usually in advance of Royal visits. In 1982, I was privileged to be asked to check out Pope John Paul II's altar before his arrival at Bellahouston Park, although another officer was charged with searching the Popemobile. It was a glorious day in June, with the sun beating down, and everyone was in good spirits. All the police officers were bantering with the crowds and it seemed amazing that one man could hold such a vast audience in his sway.

A less successful enterprise was my attempt to become a part-time diver with the underwater unit. I was asked to join because of my swimming abilities and I was keen to give it a try. But it soon became clear I suffered from what is known as 'greedy' breathing. At depths of 125 ft, and in total darkness, I would start to gulp in air and could empty a quarter of my tank very quickly. There were one or two occasions I almost didn't make it to the surface before the tank was empty, but pride kept me from giving up. Then one day, we were asked to search Loch Long for a diver who had drowned. He had gone out with two others to do a 'bounce' – diving to a depth of 125 ft and then coming straight back up again. Such manoeuvres are carried out around once a month to keep divers' logbooks up to date.

Anyway, these lads dived down together, but as they were coming back up, the middle one got his leg caught in fishing wire. He was in total darkness and his mouthpiece had come out and sprung away from him. If he had kept his cool that wouldn't have been a problem because he could have reached behind him to his tank and run his hand along the tube until he found the mouthpiece and pulled it back in. But he must have panicked because he didn't manage to do that. When his friends got to the surface, they realised he was in trouble and they went back down to try to rescue him, but by the time they got there his tank had emptied and he had drowned. It was left to us to retrieve the body. That was the last dive I did. The tragedy brought it home to me that not only was I risking my own life, but I was also risking the lives of my colleagues so I held my hands up and everyone accepted I was doing the right thing. Besides, I could get my adrenaline rush in other ways.

As more guns were finding their way onto the streets of Scotland, it gradually became obvious to Strathclyde Police that they needed a specialist firearms unit, a crack team trained to deal with hostage situations. I was lucky enough to be picked for it. We were trained in the use of .22 and .38 Smith and Wesson handguns and shotguns and shown how to operate an inner and an outer cordon at sieges; I became a Class A handgun and Class B shotgun handler. I was also used as a runner: someone who would get a telephone line or a wire into a building so the police could listen to what was being said inside or give the people inside some sort of secure communication systems. Again we were sent on training courses with guns that fired blue tack pellets. The exercises were like the 'Laser-Quest' games used for corporate teambuilding, except more serious. You would be sent to clear a room and suddenly there would be a bang and you'd feel a sharp pain and know you had been shot at from above. In the showers at night everyone would be laughing as they compared the bruises they had sustained as a result of being hit.

There were a few initial hitches over the unit's name. We were going to be called the 'Arms Intervention Detection Squad' until the newspapers realised our acronym would be 'AIDS' and the next idea was to call us the 'Fast Action Response Team' or 'FART'. The management finally settled on 'Tactical Firearms Support Unit'. These early problems were soon forgotten, however, and once we were up and running we led the way in firearms provision in Scotland and won a nationwide reputation for professionalism.

It was as a result of my firearms training that I was picked for the job, in 1985, that was to represent the peak of my time as a member of the Support Unit. The drama began when I received a phone call telling me I was needed for a job Special Branch was in charge of. I was to bring sandwiches and expect to be on call for the foreseeable future. Making my way into Springburn as quickly as possible, I switched on the radio and heard how a bomb factory had been discovered in Glasgow's Southside. Five suspects were being held in Stewart Street police station under the Prevention of Terrorism Act.

The eventual haul was considerably larger and included a list of 16 locations the IRA planned to bomb, with proposed dates pencilled in. Soon after, a booby-trapped bomb containing three-and-a-half-pounds of gelignite was found in the Rubens Hotel in Buckingham Palace Road, central London – one of the named locations. The bomb's timer was running and it would have gone off on 29 July 1985 if a bomb-disposal expert had not disabled it. In a cellar not far from the flat in Glasgow's Southside were found enough explosives for the remaining 15 bombs and several time and power units (TPUs) marked with intended locations and dates. Also in the flat, which had been rented nine days earlier, was a handbag containing a Browning automatic pistol and a false Eire passport. One of the suspects was arrested with a second Browning pistol in the waistband of his trousers. What Special Branch had uncovered was a massive bomb plot that would have resulted in devastation on an unimaginable scale.

When the unit arrived at the police station, the gaffers filled in some of the missing details. This was a high-profile operation; one of the suspects was IRA Commander Patrick Magee, who was later convicted both for his part in this operation and for his role in the Brighton bombing. There were fears that Magee would make an attempt to escape from the station and that he might come under attack from rival factions and, as a result, uniformed officers – armed only with batons – were to be replaced by the Tactical Firearms Support Unit, equipped with Smith and Wesson handguns. Marksmen armed with sniper rifles and nightsights were to be positioned on the roof. We were told the suspects were being interviewed upstairs by Special Branch and we were put on 12-hour shifts until further notice, with an hour's briefing and debriefing at either end. We were not to discuss anything we saw or heard while on duty outside of Stewart Street.

As there were so many armed officers on the premises a system had to be devised to ensure the operation was properly controlled. When your name was called out, you would go behind a curtain and receive your firearm. Then you would sign for your bullets and the officer in charge would give you your instructions for the day.

At first, I was simply standing on a corner of the street and, as the heavens opened, the novelty of guarding suspected terrorists quickly wore off. However, very soon I was told I was to be put on cell duty, along with my closest friend on the Support Unit, Joe. To this day, I am not sure why we were chosen for the task, but I think it was because we didn't take part in the office politics that led some officers to be snooty to those from other departments. We were never cliquey, we tried to establish a rapport with everyone we met and we made ourselves quite popular as a result. On top of this, Special Branch had to be sure it was picking men who would not gossip about what they had seen and Joe and I were considered trustworthy.

We soon found out we were to guard Magee himself, who was proving hard to break. One strange thing about Magee was that he didn't look particularly hard. If you had bumped into him in a pub, you'd have seen a wee Irishman with a beard and a glint in his eye; you may even have stopped to share a joke with him. He never acknowledged us when we spoke to him, just looked straight at us with a blank stare, yet from time to time we saw something that made us suspect that behind the cold façade lurked a sense of humour.

After handing in our firearms, we set up a room for ourselves in the passageway with tables and chairs; we sat and read, checking on Magee every half an hour. When Special Branch were ready to interview him, we would ask him to present himself at the cell door, check him over for any injuries and log him out. Then, after three or four hours, Special Branch would bring him back to us. This went on for a while until Special Branch informed us they were going to use psychological techniques in an attempt to disorientate him. But Magee was one of the IRA's top men and he had his own way of dealing with the stress.

Although there was no communication between us, we soon discovered Magee's coping mechanism was his bizarre washing ritual. Every day, we would take him to the metal basins in the passageway where the prisoners stripped off, and, like a compulsive obsessive, he would scrub every inch of his body. Despite the primitive conditions, he would wash every finger individually, starting at the nail and working his way down. When he had finished doing one hand, he would dry it with a paper towel and move onto the next one and so on with the rest of his body. We came to understand that this was his therapy, the way he maintained his equilibrium after hours in a 6 ft square cell and Joe and I were fascinated by it. Every now and again, we would try to wind him up by shouting: 'You've missed a bit,' but his face would never crack.

My time on cell duty, fascinating though it was, was overcast by an unrelated problem that had been simmering for some time. Months earlier, as a result of a tip-off from one of my snouts, I had been involved in a drugs raid on a house in Saracen, Glasgow. Because I did not know Saracen well, I had enlisted the cooperation of the community liaison officer, Archie, and his probationer, who helped me pull the operation together. In one sense, it had been highly successful. The property contained drugs: we recovered 50 heroin wraps, which the householder admitted were his. It was straightforward. However, as the date of the court case approached, the defendant suddenly denied that he had ever admitted being the owner of the drugs. The probationer also took fright and refused to testify, leaving Archie – a naturally nervous man – in a panic. The week I was on cell duty at Stewart Street was the week before the drugs case was to be heard at the High Court in Glasgow. I knew Archie had been trying to get hold of me, but since he was on day shift and I was on nights, we kept missing one another. The messages had gradually taken on a more pressing tone and I had put them in my pocket, fully intending to do something about them, but never quite getting around to it.

Meanwhile, the IRA suspects had started a 'dirty' strike, where they refused to wash or use the toilet facilities provided for them and instead smeared their excrement on the walls and floors of their cells; the unit bore the brunt of this strike. After Magee had been moved around a couple of times, it was decided to leave him to fester in his squalid cell so the stench was beginning to pervade every corner of the police station. Previously so hygiene-obsessed, Magee was now filthy, his hair matted with excrement, which he also daubed across his walls.

Then, towards the end of the week, before I had the chance to return any of Archie's calls, I was ushered in to a private room and told that Archie had committed suicide. It appeared that, though he clearly had other serious problems, his worries over the court case had driven him over the edge. That morning, while on duty and wearing his uniform, he had driven to a secluded spot and connected a hosepipe to the exhaust, feeding it through the window of his car.

Because the senior officers were aware of my distress, I was immediately taken off cell duty, which was perceived as stressful. With typical managerial incompetence, however, I was detailed instead to the rooftop of the multi-storey building opposite Stewart Street police office. I wasn't a marksman so couldn't be given a gun; I was just handed a nightsight and left to it. In the darkness my mind ran riot. I could hear Archie's voice urging me to phone him and I imagined him coming up behind me and pushing me over the edge. In the end, I was allowed to come back in and return to my post with Joe, and his sense of humour helped get me through the next few days.

On the day Magee was to be transferred to London, Joe came up with a wind-up to cheer me up. Half an hour before the IRA terrorist was to be taken from his cell, Joe unlocked the cell door. Holding a bucket in his hand, he said: 'Prisoner One, we've all clubbed together and brought you this to help you finish your decorating – it's a bucket of shit.' For the first time, Magee threw his head back and laughed and we knew that for a fleeting moment we had pierced his cold veneer. This flash of humanity was short-lived, however. Magee did not speak to us as he left the station and was later given eight life sentences with a recommendation he serve a minimum of 35 years for his part in the Brighton bombing, this conspiracy and other terrorist charges. In 1999, he was freed as part of the Good Friday Peace Agreement.

In later years I moved on from the unit and Joe transferred to the Dog Branch. Joe was a good mate but we lost contact over the years – as you do in the job. Much to my regret I never saw Joe again as he died while serving in the Dog Branch about four years after we both left the Support Unit.

For the most part, my time in the Support Unit went well. I proved I was capable and got good results. But I have always been unable to sit back and allow myself to be walked over and that proved to be my downfall in the end. It wasn't helped by the fact that, although I was very popular with most of my colleagues, I made one enemy, and he was determined to put the knife in my back.

The bad feeling between this man, a sergeant, and me reached its height during an operation to catch car thieves in the Gorbals. The division was having a real problem and asked the Support Unit to come in and swamp the area with uniformed officers in an attempt to scare the culprits off. I simply couldn't believe anyone was proposing to handle the operation in this way. I knew if we did that, we would simply move the problem on to another division. 'Why not go in covertly, catch the thieves and clear up the crime?' I asked. To my surprise I was taken seriously and the Inspector agreed to put six of us in plain clothes on the case. Unfortunately, the Sergeant, who had serious crime squad training but had never arrested an angry man, was put in charge of the operation. He wanted to put three men up on the roof with binoculars and three on the street, but I thought this was a ridiculous idea. If the man on the roof spotted a break-in, he would have to radio one of the men on the street and that officer would then have to race to the scene, by which time, the chances are, the thief would have moved on.

Instead, I proposed that we pull in as many guys as possible until we got some hard information, which is what we did. Eventually we were told two men – junkies – of no fixed abode were selling car radios near Glasgow Central railway station. So we knew who was responsible and we knew they were stealing from the Gorbals and then transporting their haul across the river; all we needed to do was to catch them at it. I suggested we went undercover in the most inconspicuous guise I could think of – street cleaners. The strategy worked well and we caught the thieves red-handed, but who took the credit? The Sergeant, of course. At that point it became clear to me I was being well and truly shafted.

I had already annoyed the management by going to the Scottish Police Federation because we were being deprived of our overtime payments and time off in lieu for working extra hours. As a result of standing up for my rights, I had been pegged as a troublemaker.

That undeserved reputation caused me problems when I came to requalify for my firearms certificate. The pass mark was 50 per cent and at that time I was a 78 per cent shot, which made me a good shot. On the day in question I shot 76 per cent, 2 per cent off my average. I was called in by the Chief Superintendent and told: 'We are going to take away your authorisation to hold a firearm from you until you re-qualify. You're obviously tired because of your job, so we will give you a break.' I was outraged and I wasn't able to keep quiet about it. I told him I thought I was being stitched up because I had rocked the boat with the federation.

Five days later I found out I was to be transferred out of the Support Unit and back to the division. I was due an assessment before I left and the Sergeant who despised me for showing him up carried it out. Although I was popular with my colleagues, he decided I was a bad influence, a disruptive member of the team. I couldn't believe it. After everything I had done, I would start my new job, at Easterhouse police office, with this terrible reference. I would have a black mark against my name before I stepped a foot inside the door. I vowed then and there that I would get my own back on this officer and it wasn't long before I got the chance to wreak my revenge.

5

MAKING ENEMIES AND INFORMANTS

EASTERHOUSE IS THE hardest estate in Glasgow. For three decades it has struggled to escape the shadow cast by its violent reputation, but despite its efforts its razor-gang image still hangs like a millstone round its neck. Visiting celebrities and PR campaigns alike have failed to address the problems of an area where unemployment is endemic and rival godfathers have been known to take each other out in Mafia-style executions.

In the '60s, singer Frankie Vaughan descended on Easterhouse and urged its young people to throw their knives into giant plastic bags, to give up the slashing in favour of more wholesome pastimes, but his message fell on deaf ears. Thirty years later, after the cult film *Small Faces* perpetuated the image, French President Jacques Chirac was taken round what was described as a model of urban regeneration. Certainly hundreds of thousands of pounds have been poured into improvement schemes, but the boarded-up houses and lifeless junkies – who were swept off the streets for Chirac's visit – are still what you remember most from a trip there.

When I arrived in Easterhouse in the 1980s, the scale of the deprivation appalled me, although I was far from being a rookie. Every day, the uniformed officers faced a different danger. We would walk into a close and there would be a gang lying in wait for us or we would park our car and they would try to blow it up by sticking a rag in the petrol tank and lighting it.

There was one group of teenagers who carried baseball bats with nails hammered into the ends of them so one side would be sharp and pointed and the other side would be blunt.

I endured many kickings during my time there. I had a narrow escape from a meat cleaver, which landed in the bonnet of my car yards from my fingers and I suffered a fractured sternum when I was used as a punchball while trying to sort out a domestic dispute.

The conditions inside many of the houses we visited were so appalling we had to wipe our shoes on the way out. People would allow their dogs to defecate over kitchen floors. We raided one house because we thought they were dealing drugs, only to find out it was chips, not heroin, that they were selling through their front window. They had fitted gas pipes to a giant metal bath and were using it as an enormous deep fat fryer.

In such an environment, you need a sense of solidarity and a sense of humour just to survive. But you also need to take a tough line with the people you deal with, to talk to them in a language they understand, or you will go under. Violence is the currency in Easterhouse and the surrounding estates; it's the only means of buying respect and unless you can demonstrate that you can be just as hard as the criminals you are trying to lock up you will not achieve anything. We never began our inquiries aggressively. If we could get a result by talking to the neds, then we would. Indeed, we often helped those who cooperated by securing the best deal possible for them in the circumstances. But those who had a bad attitude would see another side of us; they would feel our batons on the backs of their heads and they would realise we were in charge. The methods we used to secure convictions sometimes raised eyebrows outside the profession, but they reduced the number of burglaries suffered by law-abiding people who had invested what little money they managed to save – and for me, that made our efforts all worthwhile.

When I arrived at Easterhouse I was of course worried that the bad reference I had been given by the Sergeant in the Support Unit would affect my standing. But, within hours of arriving in the office, the Inspector took me to one side and told me he would look after me provided I gave him his money's worth; this was a great relief. There was never any doubt he would get his money's worth from me because, while many of the officers were lazy or had their eyes on a rapid promotion to a pen-pushing post in headquarters, I was genuinely interested in solving crimes. Where others were content to firefight, to tackle each breach of the peace as it happened, I wanted to take a more proactive approach, to catch some of the burglars and drug dealers, instead of handing all the important cases upstairs to the Criminal Investigation Department (CID).

I was helped in this ambition when I teamed up with an enthusiastic young probationer from a similar background to myself – an ex-Army cadet called John. The Easterhouse *Starsky and Hutch* were born. John and I worked together for three and a half years. We kicked in doors, cultivated informants and got results.

The first tout (informant) we signed up was a prolific burglar. We had been called out to house after house, where the thief had broken in through a window. Although it was clear the same man was committing all the burglaries, we had no idea who we were looking for, until finally one of the victims gave us a name. But instead of setting up surveillance, John and I hatched a plan. We looked out for the miscreant while patrolling in our car and when we spotted him walking along the street we hijacked him, taking him for a run to an opencast mine. The burglar could not believe what was happening. We ignored his protests and kept driving up a dirt track until we arrived in a yard guarded by two snarling Alsatians. There, we stopped the car and explained the deal. We told the man we knew he had been committing the burglaries in the division and that a jail sentence was inevitable in the long term. But we said we would take no further action if he signed himself on as our informant and started turning in other criminals, such as drugs dealers. But he wouldn't cooperate so we opened the car doors, forced him out and drove off, leaving him to the dogs. The last we saw of him, the Alsatians were only inches behind him, snapping at his ankles.

A week later, when we were on late shift, we saw him hobbling along the road. He flagged down our car and said: 'Yous are a pair of mad bastards. But I would rather work with you than against you.' He needed eight stitches in his backside, but our punishment had paid dividends. He signed himself on as our first informant. The burglaries went down because he moved his operation into another division and he gave us good information on other criminals. We didn't do him any favours in return. We circulated his details to other police offices, and he was frequently arrested, but they could never break him during interviews and he remained at large despite our efforts.

The more informants we signed on, the more hits we scored. We were making dozens of arrests every week and forging a reputation for ourselves amongst our colleagues. Most of the time, our successes were based on old-fashioned police work, on building up a network of contacts and following up tips. But from time to time we were prepared to cross the line in the cause of justice.

On one occasion, we were called out to a car hit and run, in which an old man had lost a leg. An informant told us the name of the driver and said he had hidden his car in a lock-up because he was afraid forensics would get their hands on it. We arrested the man, but he was completely uncooperative. I lost my temper and we ended up in a boxing match and he suffered a sore jaw. In the end he held his hands up and took us to the lock-up. We may have bent the rules slightly, but the only way we would have found that car was by causing him to break down and tell us where it was. As a result, the hit-and-run criminal was jailed for five years and the old man received criminal compensation.

The other side of the job, the side that justified our hard work, was the gratitude we so often received from the community. Mothers would come in and thank us for locking up their junkie sons because the jail sentence had led them to kick the habit; those who had all their jewellery stolen would be overjoyed to get it back. In return we got involved with the community by doing sponsored runs to raise money for local charities and by visiting the local schools, advising the youngsters and staff in respect of anti-drugs campaigns.

Our achievements were praised by our superiors who basked in reflected glory, but they were attracting rather less welcome attention from other sources. We were a constant irritant to the criminal fraternity because we were curtailing their activities and to the CID because we were showing them up.

We were not going to be allowed to make such an impact on Easterhouse unchallenged. The thugs we arrested started filing complaints against us almost as a matter of course. Some of the allegations made against us were patently ludicrous. They would say, for example, that we had threatened to inject them with a dirty needle unless they told us what we wanted to hear or that we had tied them up, tortured them or even thrown them off bridges prior to bringing them in. But, however incredible the claims, their solicitors would take them on board. As a result, we were frequently visited by the discipline department or 'rubber-heel brigade'. Around 30 complaints were made against me, although none of the charges were ever substantiated. I can honestly say I never fitted anyone up during my time there and not a single discipline charge was laid against me. On the other hand, I did receive many commendations for my work.

The hostility from CID was just as tangible. The detectives felt we were treading on their toes and were clearly wary about our methods. At every morning conference the uniform inspectors would gloat about our latest arrests, rubbing their noses in our successes. I think my partnership with John probably set back my career about three years. CID didn't want me as a detective because they thought it would be too difficult to tame me. Looking back, they were probably right. I did need to calm down, but I was getting an amazing kick out of my work, and it was a learning experience I think I had to go through in order to progress.

To add to my troubles, within months of my arrival the Sergeant responsible for my downfall in the Support Unit had been transferred to Easterhouse. By then, I was already an established member of the team, but this did nothing to quell the hostility I felt for him. Soon after he arrived, he suggested we 'bury the hatchet', but I wanted to get even before I was prepared to put the whole thing behind me. For months I had to watch my back as he checked and rechecked my work, looking for mistakes that might bring me down. Every time I moved he seemed to be behind me with some whinge about the way I worked. In particular, he was obsessed by the fact that John and I did not always wear our hats in the patrol cars. It wasn't a big deal; it was just that as you ran headlong into yet another fight, your dress code wasn't your first concern.

One night, we were called to a serious disturbance in a close, and forgot to put on our hats before tackling it. After arresting the troublemakers, we headed back to our car, only to find our caps had disappeared. At first we suspected local teenagers, but when we asked a passer-by if he had seen anything, he said he he one of our officers had taken them away. I couldn't believe it. Not only was the Sergeant childish enough to pull this stupid stunt, but he had done it while we were facing danger close by.

When we got back to the office, we waited until the tea break and then sneaked into his office. Our hats were in his bottom drawer so we took them back and then locked all his drawers and cabinets before throwing his keys into a nearby Loch. As everyone turned up in their casual clothes to sign off that night, we turned up very pointedly in our hats so he could be under no misapprehension as to who had stolen his keys. He was livid, but he couldn't accuse us of anything because to do so he would have to admit to stealing our hats. It took him hours to sort out the problem but he never mentioned his troubles to us and from then on relations between us warmed slightly.

Simultaneously, relations with my wife were cooling down. I was obsessed with my work and I was not spending any more time with her and the girls. Lindsey had not always encouraged me in my career and so I sometimes felt she was holding me back. Now, though, she has a high-flying job with the BBC and I realise it works both ways.

On the strength of the extra hours I worked during the Miners' Strike, we had moved into a big detached house, but it wasn't long before I ran into financial trouble. As the overtime dried up I found myself running up an overdraft as I waited desperately for every salary cheque to arrive. To help out, Lindsey took a job as a wages clerk with the Development Corporation and we began living largely separate lives. Things did not improve between us when I finally got asked to join the CID and, only 18 months into my career as a detective, we finally split up. Soon afterwards, I met my second wife, Wendy – also a police officer – through our work. I still see my girls on a regular basis.

When the call came for me to exchange my uniform for a detective's suit, I was not to be posted as I had anticipated, at Easterhouse, where the bad blood continued, but at Kirkintilloch, a middle-class town outside Glasgow, and then almost immediately to Bishopbriggs. In 1986, I began as an aide to CID, which simply means you are only there on a trial basis until the bosses see if you are going to make the grade.

Bishopbriggs was a strange place to work because on the one hand the people who lived there were all well-heeled with large houses. On the other hand, however, it attracted travelling scumbags from all the surrounding estates – Maryhill, Saracen, Springburn and even Easterhouse – so burglaries were rife.

At first it was mostly burglaries I was dealing with, which was familiar territory to me. I was privileged to work alongside a police sergeant called Mick. Although he was later accused, along with a number of other officers, of taking backhanders from one of Glasgow's foremost gangsters, I never saw Mick put a foot wrong. The allegations against him were fully investigated by another police force although it was some years later before Mick was informed that the allegations were deemed to be unfounded and malicious. Mick was later promoted and is now a chief inspector in Strathclyde. Unfortunately, the allegations held back Mick's career progression as he should have reached the dizzy heights of chief superintendent – he is certainly more than capable of the duties required by this rank. Criminals often use the complaints procedure as a way to muddy the waters and cause unnecessary grief to police officers and their families and Mick was a victim of this.

Mick was 100% police officer and served as my role model. He was the same height as me, with jet-black hair and he looked like a boxer. He mixed easily with the neds but he played a shrewd game. If we were targeting a team of burglars, he would have two of them signed on as informants. That way, if one of the snouts held back on vital information, he would still be able to catch the burglars red-handed. The renegade informer would be arrested along with the others as a warning to give the whole story the next time. Mick and three others, including myself, formed ourselves into a team to tackle the house-breakings and when they subsided, we moved onto drugs. We signed on those we caught driving while disqualified as snouts and they led us to a string of excellent convictions.

In the time I was at Bishopbriggs there was only one killing but it made a deep impression on me. It involved a budding young footballer, on an S-form for Celtic (an S-form provides a commitment from the club to young players), who was stabbed during a fight on grassed land in the town. The story we were told was that he had challenged another teenager to a fight and lent forward into the knife his rival was holding up in self-defence. By the time we arrived the victim had been taken to hospital where he was certified dead on arrival and the murder case was moved to Baird Street in the city centre.

It was left to me to break the news to the boy's parents. I will never forget the anguish on their faces as I told them he was dead. They just could not believe their talented son could ever have been involved in such an incident. In the years that followed, I dealt with many bereaved parents, but I was never touched so deeply again.

My Kirkintilloch career spanned two years, during which time I was officially appointed a detective constable. I was to return to the Scottish Police College at Tulliallan for a residential period of eight weeks, this time for Detective training. This was a different Tulliallan from my original training some years earlier; now I was attending as an experienced police officer, being given respect by the young rookies who embarrassingly constantly called me sir. One of the most valuable lessons I was to learn on the course was how to conduct a successful interrogation. We were taught not only about procedures, which had been tightened up shortly before I joined in the face of miscarriage of justice cases in England, but also about psychology. In particular, we were taught how to pick up on the body language of the interviewee and use it to your advantage; we were instructed on how to tell when the suspect is lying, not from what he says, but from how he moves. If he repeats your question, we were told that he is buying time; if he looks up at the ceiling he is rehearsing his story before saying the words out loud; if he avoids eye contact then he is afraid he will be caught out.

I also learned that the 'nice police officer/nasty police officer' routine, or 'sweet and sour', as we called it, was not just a myth from situation comedies, but a means of unsettling the suspect, to make him more likely to confess. The nasty police officer will use aggression to intimidate the suspect, making him more susceptible to the kindness of his counterpart. When the nice police officer moves in with his reassuring voice and body language, he is likely to gain his trust quite easily. On all occasions you would try to talk to the interviewee in his own language and on his level. The technique sounds simple, but had to be employed quite subtly to be effective. And since, fortunately, the introduction of tape recorders meant any other method of extracting confessions was a thing of the past, it had to be perfected.

Once again, the rate at which we were securing convictions in Bishopbriggs meant we were attracting hostility from lawyers whose clients we were locking up. Some of them would do anything the defendants wanted in an attempt to convince them they were getting their money's worth. If they could cast doubt on the way an identity parade or an interview had been handled then they would.

Once I was hauled up for allegedly discussing a case with a fellow witness in a court lift, when in fact I had been doing nothing of the sort. In fact we had exchanged a few words about a case neither of us was remotely involved in. The other witness corroborated my version of events in court, but the solicitor had succeeded in muddying the waters as far as the jury was concerned and so achieved his aim. Partly because of the complaints and partly because Mick and I were such good operators, the management thought they ought to split us up and double our impact. I was soon moved to Baird Street – a busy divisional headquarters in the city centre.

At Baird Street we dealt with 14 killings in a single year and clocked up far more experience than Kirkintilloch could ever have afforded us. Perhaps the most disturbing was the death of a three-year-old boy, who died in his bath in Roystonhill. The boy's uncle, who had been looking after the toddler, claimed his nephew had drowned when he left the room for a few minutes. He insisted he had come back in to find him floating face down, but something about his story did not ring true. The uncle was a notorious junkie and when we arrived and discovered he had cleaned the bath before calling us, our suspicions were immediately aroused. Instead of what the uncle told us, we believed the little boy's head had been held under the water as he was being sexually assaulted.

The uncle was arrested and a child-abuse specialist was called in to oversee the post-mortem examination, which seemed to confirm our worst fear: the toddler appeared to have been tampered with. However, somewhere between the first autopsy and the one carried out by the defence, the physical evidence that proved the abuse was lost, although we never found out who was to blame. To our horror, the case against the uncle was dropped. Our only consolation was that he died a few years later of a drugs overdose.

One of the benefits of working at Baird Street was the presence of a streetwise detective inspector by the name of Willie. Like the hero of William McIlvanney's *Laidlaw* books, Willie was a complex, brusque man. But he was so good at his job you would never challenge him even if you temporarily doubted his sanity.

The best example of Willie's talents was when he was in charge of the inquiry into the killing of Joseph Conroy, who died in a fight in a bloodbath up a close in Roystonhill. At first the killing seemed quite straightforward: two men, possibly three, chased Conroy along the road and into the close before stabbing him to death. Although we had no leads as to the identity of the attacker, and being in Roystonhill we were unlikely to be given any pointers by the local residents, it seemed clear it was part of an ongoing war over drugs and territory. Eventually our informants came up with some names and we were well on our way to charging those we believed were responsible. But just when it seemed we were on the brink of a result, Willie strode into the office and told us to start again from the beginning. After shutting down the 30-strong inquiry team and handpicking a few trusted cohorts, Willie told us the guilty man was James Welsh, a drug dealer from a large Glasgow family. None of us doubted Welsh was capable of killing Conroy, but we knew of no connection between the two. However, Willie declined to enlighten us further, insisting it was up to us to find the evidence that would convict him. At first it was difficult to find Welsh, who had gone underground, but eventually we tracked him down and brought him in for interview. He told us that on the night of the killing he was staying in a hotel in Blackpool with his wife and children, arriving there at 6 p.m. on Friday and staying overnight, which gave him the perfect alibi for a crime committed 300 miles away and three hours later. Welsh swore his wife would vouch for him, which she did, giving us a carbon copy of his story. Our only option was to travel down to Blackpool and put some pressure on the owner of the hotel – a sleazy, hole-in-the-wall establishment down a shady side street.

The owner, an old lag with a fag dangling from his mouth, showed us the register book, which bore Welsh's name and the date. But in trying to cover his own back, Welsh had tripped up, writing 'Friday, 19' instead of 'Friday, 18'. It was a small discrepancy, but enough to suggest we were after all on the right trail.

We soon discovered the hotel owner was a former armed robber who had invested his money and was now going straight. When we found that he would not cooperate we took him back to Glasgow with us for further questioning. Finally he cracked and told us everything. Welsh had arrived at the hotel on the Saturday and given the hotel owner some money in return for falsifying the entry in the register.

The next stage was to bring Welsh back in for interview. Willie started to caution him as expected, but then, before we knew it, he went straight into the murder charge. I don't know who was the most shocked: Welsh, his solicitor or the detectives. We thought the Inspector was taking a terrible chance because we did not have all the loose ends tied up. But as Welsh approached the charge bar, Willie stepped forward like Hercule Poirot in the denouement of an Agatha Christie thriller and ordered him to roll his right sleeve up. Gradually a scar with three homemade stitches emerged from underneath the sleeve. Then Willie explained why he had been so confident of Welsh's guilt. During the inquiry, a snout had tipped him off that Welsh had injured his arm and was claiming it had happened while fitting a carpet. Forensics had taken blood samples from the scene of the killing and some of these had matched Welsh's. However, this in itself was not enough – Willie had needed us to find the evidence to make a case against him and we had succeeded.

It turned out the fight had been over drugs as we had originally suspected. Conroy's team had ripped off Welsh's team and Welsh's team had gone out for revenge. Although Conroy had a blade, the others took it from him and used it against him. Welsh was sentenced to 13 years and it was all because of Willie's detective skills and determination.

The experience I gained from these inquiries was important: it taught me when to bend the rules and when to play by the book and it taught me never to make assumptions. With several years as a detective – and some of the most gruesome cases the force has ever witnessed – behind me, I must have thought there were few surprises left in CID.

But nothing could have prepared me for the murder of Arthur Thompson junior, the son of Glasgow's Godfather, which ripped the city's underworld apart.

6

THE BIG BOYS' LEAGUE

AS I WAS carving a reputation for myself in the police force, two or three men who served their apprenticeship on the other side of the fence were also graduating with honours. In the criminal fraternity, as in any cut-throat organisation, only the most intelligent or ruthless distinguish themselves from the legions of wannabes and it is these who would enter the premier division of Glasgow's underworld. In the '80s and early '90s a handful of those high achievers were jostling for position with the old guard. As a result of their merciless approach to their rivals, and the connections they made with gangsters in other parts of the country, they had gained a degree of notoriety and were emerging as the key players in the city's thriving criminal empires.

Although for much of the time the various teams within the city operated in tandem, respecting each other's territory, there were sporadic turf wars characterised by tit-for-tat shootings, with kneecappings a popular form of warning or 'frightener'.

In the early '80s, the focus for these turf wars was the ice cream vans that toured the estates selling sweets and cigarettes stolen in bulk. So lucrative were these rounds that those who owned their own vehicles, buying stock from firms like Fifti Ices, or leased their vans from companies such as the Marchetti Brothers, fought tooth and nail to protect their patch from invaders. Ice cream vans were frequently stoned or had their tyres slashed as they crossed into each other's pitches in the hopes of increasing their profits. Those who served through the hatches often risked their lives, the windows of their vans prone to being blasted by a shotgun or blown out by a firebomb.

The Ice Cream Wars, at first the butt of comedians' jokes, were to reach a tragic conclusion with the murder of six members of the Doyle family, including a baby, in an arson attack on their Ruchazie home in 1984. One of the Doyles – 18-year-old Andrew – had been given a Marchetti van rent-free in an attempt to freeze out the competition, and it is thought the fire was supposed to warn him off. But the petrol poured through the family's front door was absorbed into the carpet and the flat was rapidly engulfed in flames. One of Glasgow's leading criminal figures was Tam McGraw. McGraw was a member of the Barlanark team (a gang of house breakers), ran his own ice cream van and was among those charged with murder. However these charges were later dropped. Instead, Thomas (TC) Campbell, also of the Barlanark team, and an acquaintance, Joe Steele, were jailed for life for the offence, although they have always maintained their innocence and are continuing in their campaign for an appeal. There were others who were just as deeply involved, who successfully evaded justice.

Whatever his role or otherwise in the Ice Cream Wars, McGraw was one of the city's sharpest criminals, whose ability to manipulate those around him made him virtually untouchable. One of the founding members of the Barlanark team, he was shrewd enough to invest his money in a beautiful house, an ice cream van and a taxi firm, instead of squandering it on cigarettes and alcohol as so many other thieves and robbers do. Latterly, he bought a string of pubs, earning himself the nickname 'The Licensee' amongst his peers. But it wasn't just his ability to present himself as a legitimate businessman that allowed McGraw to evade capture for so long. In later years it was to be claimed by a rival, Tam Bagan, in an official complaint via his solicitor to the chief constable, that McGraw had a number of police officers in his pocket, and that one of those police officers was Mick, the Detective Sergeant I worked with at Bishopbriggs. It was a myth McGraw perpetuated when it suited him. It was said McGraw was willing to betray other criminals or to hand over guns in return for favours rendered and those terms were acceptable if the deal as a whole was in the public interest. For example, on one occasion it was purported he would lead the police to a weapons cache if they would sort out his friend's traffic charges, which apparently they did with the help of the procurator fiscal. We always suspected McGraw had access to guns, but we could never prove it. However, it was better that some of them should be taken out of circulation, no questions asked, than that they should remain in the hands of gangsters because of a misplaced sense of integrity.

McGraw's stature in Glasgow's underworld remained largely unchallenged until Tam Bagan made his claims about police corruption and his rival's role as an informer. Since then, despite a recent acquittal on conspiracy-to-supply charges, McGraw's power has rapidly diminished as friends and enemies alike wonder if he has been responsible for grassing them up. Although he has undoubtedly been powerful, McGraw only took on the mantle of Glasgow's Godfather for a short period after the Thompson dynasty ended in 1993 with the death of old Arthur from a heart attack.

Like McGraw, Arthur Thompson senior was one of the old school and had been a notorious Glasgow East End gangster as far back as the '50s. He started out associating with thieves and robbers, but he networked so well that, by the time his son was murdered, his tentacles reached all over the UK. He travelled to London frequently to 'sort people out' and often boasted about his friendship with the Krays. Yet despite his notoriety, he had surprisingly few convictions, the last of which he received as far back as 1968. Early in his career he served sentences for extortion, assault and robbery but he was acquitted of the only murder charges he ever faced (he was accused of driving his Jaguar into a van containing two rivals and forcing them off the road) before pronouncing himself a 'legitimate businessman'.

Thompson was a Mafia-style godfather, although he disliked the sobriquet and ruled both through fear and because he provoked a kind of grudging respect in those around him. He lived on Provanmill Road in Blackhill, in an overblown house which he called 'Villa Ponderosa', but others dubbed 'Southfork'. Made out of two council houses, plus extensions, with four chimney pots and two satellite dishes and extensive security systems, the house dominated the street and was accompanied by a second property a few doors up that he had converted for his son Arthur junior. A holiday home in Rothesay and a villa in Spain completed the property register.

Thompson survived at least three attempts on his own life but was a jinx on all around him. His mother-in-law, Margaret Johnstone, was killed when a bomb exploded under his car in 1966, three months after his acquittal on the murder charges, while his daughter, Margaret, died of a heroin overdose in 1989, prompting her addict boyfriend to flee the country to escape the consequences. When Thompson himself was attacked, he refused to cooperate with the police investigation in any way. On one occasion, after doctors removed a bullet from Thompson's stomach, he continued to insist it was a drill bit that came off during home improvements.

Like most Mafia bosses, Thompson wanted his son to be his heir, someone who would be able to take over the family business when he decided to bow out. Arthur junior, however, was an altogether less-competent criminal. He served an eight-year prison sentence in Shotts and Peterhead after the drugs sqaud caught him in possession of heroin. Overweight and boastful, he was extremely unpopular with the other inmates who would spit into his food. His enforced diet of chocolate earned him the nicknames 'Fat Boy' and 'The Mars Bar Kid' among those who knew him although they would never have been so bold as to use the nicknames to his face. Arthur junior would not have appreciated the joke.

In his son's absence, Thompson senior found himself increasingly reliant on eager young upstarts like Paul Ferris and Tam Bagan to look after the 'business' in Scotland while he was down south. In particular, it was said, he used Ferris and Bagan to act as heavies and collect his debts.

Ferris suffered from delusions of grandeur and was dangerously unpredictable. As he got a taste for the high living, the flash cars and the designer suits he became increasingly ambitious. Despite warnings from people like McGraw about the consequences of such action, Ferris and Bagan decided to make a break and set up in business for themselves – in competition with their former mentor. Ferris began recruiting his own team, people like Joe 'Bananas' Hanlon, Bobby Glover and John 'Jonah' Mackenzie, who were rumoured to have carried out armed robberies all over the country. Ferris was a violent man, but to a certain extent the aura of danger he created around himself was the result of his not inconsiderable gift for PR.

Ferris saw an opportunity to claw his way out of desperate circumstances. Despite lacking any formal education, he was intelligent and articulate. He made himself accessible to journalists, who lapped up the chance to gain an insight into a world normally denied them, becoming something of a gangster celebrity. The hype was accentuated by police officers who told apocryphal stories about their encounters with the hard man that passed into legend. I remember when I was in the Support Unit hearing intelligence reports that Ferris was threatening to kill a police officer, which may or may not have been true. What certainly wasn't true was that he was wired and tape-recording interviews when he was stopped by police – yet that rumour went around as a result of the kind of Chinese whispers Ferris seemed to set in motion. Indeed, such was the hysteria surrounding Ferris that if he visited a pub more than once the word would go round that he'd bought it. Ferris, of course, thrived on the attention and used it to his advantage to increase his standing in the criminal fraternity.

This was, broadly speaking, the lie of the land in Glasgow's underworld before the murder of Arthur Thompson junior, a murder that would unleash a fresh wave of violence onto the streets and see Ferris facing a murder charge in one of the most sensational trials of the decade.

In the months leading up to the murder, there had been an escalation of violence, particularly in Blackhill, where a series of shootings bore the hallmarks of payoffs for debts unpaid or liberties taken. Ferris's name kept surfacing. We were used to his name coming up in connection with all sorts of crimes and there was no evidence to substantiate his involvement with these ones. Later it would emerge there had also been a kneecapping on the A77 near Kilmarnock in May 1991, but the officers at Baird Street CID knew nothing about it, and even if we had there would have been no reason for us to link it with offences committed in Glasgow.

The first real sign of a turf war in the city was when we were called to a hit and run in Provanmill Road a year earlier in May 1990. When we got there it looked as though a car had mounted the kerb, ripping up a fence as it went. There was no sign of the victim, but we quickly learned the vehicle had hit Arthur Thompson (senior) from behind before reversing twice over his body. Thompson had been carried bleeding to his home by members of his family, who then took him to hospital.

Witnesses told us he had been hit by a white car, but Thompson himself was saying nothing. His injuries were not critical and he was soon released from hospital.

Then in August 1991, Arthur junior was murdered, unleashing a tide of violence. He had been serving the tail-end of his sentence in Noranside open prison near Perth, after turning down the same opportunity at Dungavel, apparently because he feared he would not last long on the outside. One of the benefits of being at Noranside was that, after a month or so, inmates were allowed home on weekend licence, but it was a perk Thompson was not to enjoy for long. On his first weekend home, he was walking the short distance from his father's house to his front door, after a meal out, when a man jumped out of a parked car and shot him three times in the back. He fell to the ground and the car was driven off at high speed. Hearing the gunfire, his father rushed out of his house. He drove Arthur junior to Glasgow Royal Infirmary, but it was too late to save his life. Arthur senior appeared to dote on his son, but he was a hard, hard man. Later in the inquiry, when I was responsible for handing him the death certificate, I was greeted by a blank, staring face. At that moment I thought back to the distress of the mother and father who lost their talented teenage son in Bishopbriggs and I realised how a life on the edge can strip you of human emotions. Earlier, at the hospital, Arthur junior's brother Billy had started to say something to the police when his father intervened, gesturing to him to 'zip' his lips.

On the morning of Arthur junior's death, I was one of 30 police officers called in to an incident room set up at Baird Street. A fellow officer and I were appointed as production officers, responsible for logging and labelling every piece of evidence or tape-recorded interview. It was clear this was going to be a complex investigation so the HOLMES (Home Office Large Major Enquiry System) computer was brought into action. At first, Russell and I were stuck in the office, dealing with forensic material such as the bullets, blood and other items from the scene. But, because the inquiry team was bringing in no more evidence for us to collate, and because we knew the Blackhill area well, we were soon pulled on to the main inquiry team.

Even at this early stage, Paul Ferris was the prime suspect, due to rumours of the hostility that had been brewing between the two camps, but we had no witnesses or forensic evidence to link him to the crime. Our first job was to try to trace the car that had been used in the shooting. Russell and I trailed round the likely car dealers but our job was hampered by the fact that Thompson senior had been round before us. It was the same everywhere we went. When the dealers realised whose son it was that had been murdered, they clammed up. It was very demoralising to be stonewalled at every juncture.

The first real break the inquiry team had was Willie Gillen, the man who had been kneecapped in Kilmarnock. Gillen had previously refused to reveal the identity of his assailant, but with a little persuasion from the inquiry team, who told him they were out to get Ferris for Arthur junior's murder, he had a change of heart and agreed to give evidence against him. He told officers he had been travelling towards Kilmarnock in a car with Ferris and Bobby Glover when Ferris pulled over and ordered him to get out. Accusing Gillen of having ripped him off, Ferris was alleged to have pulled a handgun from his pocket and kneecapped him, before leaving him seriously injured in a lay-by. In exchange for witness protection, he was now willing to tell this story in court.

At the same time, we targeted an Irish junkie, known as 'wee Barney'. Barney lived on Provanmill Road and was known for playing the Thompson camp off against the Ferris camp and vice versa. We were sure he would have relevant information and knew his habit would make him vulnerable to persuasion, so we brought him in. We told him Gillen had already agreed to testify and he quickly followed suit, confessing he was a runner for Ferris, supplying or hiding guns in exchange for money or drugs.

By now the intelligence we had suggested there were three people in the car on the night of the murder – Ferris, Glover and Hanlon – and that the vehicle had been stolen for them by a prolific car thief called Davey Logue. Davey was in hiding, but a CID team was sent out to hunt him down and, when they found him, he cracked and spilled out his version of the story. He insisted that, on Ferris's instruction, he had gone to a Lanarkshire railway station and stolen a Nissan Bluebird for a 'job'. Hours later, without being told what the job involved, he was instructed to get rid of the vehicle so he took it away and torched it. Davey knew that if he refused to cooperate he would be charged as an accessory to murder so he too agreed to give evidence against Ferris. The XR3 we understood to have been involved in the hit and run of Arthur Senior was also traced. It had been repaired and re-registered under another number. The man who owned it claimed he had bought it from Ferris. Those in charge of the inquiry felt a strong case was building up against him so they applied for and were granted a warrant for his arrest by the procurator fiscal. We knew he was due to appear before Hamilton Sheriff Court on road-traffic charges so we turned up on that date to pull him in. He was interviewed in connection with the Thompson murder as well as with the kneecapping, but he was only charged with the kneecapping. Bobby Glover was also charged with the same offence and the pair were remanded in custody in Barlinnie prison.

Russell and I, who had had numerous encounters with Paul Ferris over the years, were given the task of escorting him to Kilmarnock Sheriff Court for his judicial examination on the Gillen shooting. We immediately gained an insight into his complex character. On his way down, he was charm personified: a likeable rogue, full of smirks, one-liners and backchat, but respectful. He put on a posh west of Scotland accent and tried to pump us for information but it was all very good-natured. During the journey from Glasgow's Barlinnie Prison I saw both sides of the fence. I saw seated between Russell and myself a young man, whose life could have been mine had I not decided to stay on the right side of that fence. I could, in a sad way, relate to this guy's lifestyle. I did not agree with what he was doing but I knew it could have been me sitting there.

When we got to Kilmarnock police station and began a routine search, his personality changed and he became a vicious animal. 'Why are you taking my belt off me, you filthy polis bastards?' he shouted. 'You know who I am. You know I'm not going to injure myself.' As with every prisoner, we confiscated everything: his shoelaces, his cigarette lighter, his matches and a bundle of hand-written notes we found in one of his pockets. This was a statement he intended to read out in his defence and was extremely useful to us for intelligence purposes so we took it straight to a photocopier. By this time Ferris was spitting blood and it took three of us to march him down the corridor to the cells. As we threw him in he turned to me and shouted: 'You're a fucking Easter egg on legs, Mr Corbett!' – a reference to my short height and, at that time, overweight condition. All the other officers howled with laughter and it became a standing joke for the rest of the inquiry.

Ferris and Glover had been placed in neighbouring cells and we were positioned outside to eavesdrop on them. Neither Ferris nor Glover were stupid, however, and their conversation was vetted for our ears; they spoke of how they were being fitted up and how we didn't have as much evidence against them as we were making out.

But then suddenly the weirdest thing happened. Through the corridor echoed a soulful voice singing the gangster ballad 'Mack the Knife'. Bobby Glover may have been a vicious thug, but he performed every verse, word and note perfectly, in a strong tenor voice. It was the eeriest, most haunting thing I have ever heard, particularly in retrospect, knowing his life was so soon to end. Even today, I can't hear that song without it conjuring up the image of hard man Glover and his moving swansong.

The mood was only broken when Ferris started complaining that his defence papers had been taken away from him. Against our wishes, the duty officer quickly backed down and handed them over, but then Ferris claimed page 22 was missing. As I was the one that had taken the papers from him, I was the one that was in the frame although someone else had photocopied it. Ferris made an official complaint and an internal inquiry, known as the Page 22 Inquiry, was launched and the other officer and I were both interviewed at length. Forensic tests were carried out on the pages by handwriting and forensic experts and it was quickly proved that page 21 ran into page 23, putting me in the clear. But the accusation meant I wasn't allowed to escort Ferris back to Barlinnie where he was still being held.

The evidence against Glover on the Gillen shooting was admittedly flimsy and he was released on bail pending further court appearances. But it would have been better for Glover if he had been kept inside for his own protection. The day after he walked free from prison, just hours before Arthur Thompson junior was due to be buried, Russell and I were called to a Ford Orion saloon car in Shettleston in which Glover and Hanlon lay slaughtered. The pair were said to be part of the Barlanark team and to have been vying with Thompson junior for a bigger share of the lucrative drugs market. Hanlon, just 23, was a head case: a prolific slasher. In the year leading up to the murder, his ice cream van had been petrol bombed and he had been shot in the penis. Glover was more of a smoothie, but just as dangerous. The pair had reportedly carried out a succession of armed robberies – joint ventures involving shotguns and building societies or banks. But their pasts did not make their execution any less shocking. I was there when the bodies were taken out of the car. Glover was laid across the floor in the back of the car, tucked in behind the seats, while Hanlon was almost stuffed into the front footwell, crumpled up in a heap. They appeared to have been shot at point-blank range, one of them through the back of the head. It was the most appalling slaughter. We felt as if we must have been transported to Harlem. This Mafia-style violence could not be exploding on the streets of Glasgow. The management quickly realised that, although the two cases were very obviously connected, we would need two separate inquiries, carried out side by side so every piece of evidence could be cross-referenced.

More detectives, including whole surveillance teams, were brought in and we moved lock stock and barrel from Baird Street to a bigger office in London Road where we took over the whole of the top floor and used half of it for each inquiry. Russell and I were given a small room in which to organise the productions, which, by the end of the inquiry, totalled more than 800. The pressure was on us because by now Ferris had been charged with murdering Arthur junior and was serving his 110 days. In Scotland, this is the length of time a defendant can be held in custody between his full committal and his trial. If the Crown Office cannot get a case together before the egg timer runs out, it must drop the charges and allow the defendant to go free.

On top of my production duties, I was asked if I would join a team of officers travelling down to London to check out leads or tie up loose ends. Some of the officers were told to track down a father and son who had given Ferris an alibi for the night of the Thompson murder. I was told to go to see a *Sun* photographer who had taken pictures of Ferris while he was in London and to interview people whose cars had been seen in the vicinity of the Ford Orion on the night Hanlon and Glover were shot. It was basic police work: trace, interview and eliminate, and it threw up no fresh leads.

At the same time, the Glover/Hanlon inquiry team sent four officers down to try to trace a man called Willie Lobban, a transvestite said to have been the last person to speak to Glover and who was therefore the prime suspect.

Lobban was an associate of Ferris's and had been involved in a robbery at the Pipe Rack, a pub in Glasgow's East End. The story went that, on the night of the double murder, Glover had received a telephone call from a man called Gary saying his mother was ill and asking him to go to his house as quickly as possible. Glover's wife Irene had told police that this man, the last person to contact him on the night of his death, had arranged to meet Hanlon and him in a bar in Shettleston. The police firmly believed the man in question was Willie Lobban, who often used the alias Gary McMillan. Lobban was already on the run after absconding from Dungavel prison where he had just three months of a six-year sentence for armed robbery left to serve.

CID were trying to keep the two inquiries separate, but when they arrested Lobban in Victoria Station after receiving a tip-off, and he was prepared to say absolutely nothing, they knew they would need all the help they could get and we got roped in.

It was imperative that officers track down Lobban's house as, if he was the guilty man, there might be vital forensic evidence inside – a firearm or on bloodstained clothing. However, when they searched him, a Yale key and a return ticket to Earls Court were the only clues. These were a point in the right direction but not a great deal of help, as Earls Court was bed-sit land – full of huge buildings, each with multiple tenancies. The first thing we did was to take the key to a locksmith, who told us that there were hundreds of thousands of those kinds of locks in the area. So, while other officers were checking all the gay bars for leads, my colleague Irene and I were tasked with coordinating a mammoth lock-testing operation. We put a street map of Earls Court up in a small incident room in nearby Kensington police station and divided into small, manageable sections. Then we got 40 of the keys cut and handed them out to every officer we could find. Squads of us descended on the streets, trying the key in the lock of every door we came to. When the shift was over we would go back to the incident room and cross the streets we had tried off on the map.

This went on for two weeks. Irene and I would tramp the streets in the pouring rain for eight to ten hours, before heading back dejected. By then we were so demoralised that when, one day when we hadn't had a break, Irene said she was going for a quick wash and blow dry, I was only too happy to take the opportunity to head to the pub for a quick pint. When I got in there, however, I realised I didn't have any money so I turned tail. Irene had been unable to get a hair appointment and, as we both headed back, we bumped into each other on the street, directly outside an agency which sub-let bed-sits; guided by fate, we popped inside. It was a tiny place, just like a taxi office, but with cards advertising bed-sits in the window. We asked the man if he had let a flat recently to anyone answering Lobban's description and he just laughed in our face. 'We sub-let thousands of flats. How would I remember any one in particular?' he said. Still, we kept him talking and eventually he looked at Lobban's photograph and said yes, he did know him. Not only had he rented him a flat, but he had also asked him to help him out with odd jobs. We couldn't believe our luck. After trying literally thousands of doors, we had eventually stumbled across Lobban's flat by chance. The man took us straight round and we sealed it off as if it were a murder scene and scoured every inch of it for forensic evidence. Every single thing he owned was photographed and fingerprinted before being sent back to Glasgow for further tests. But all our efforts were in vain. There was nothing incriminating in the flat at all. We later discovered

Lobban had left Glasgow in a hurry, leaving most of his possessions behind and travelling down on a mountain bike.

He was never charged with any offence in relation to the murders of Glover and Hanlon, but he was one of three men named by Ferris as Arthur junior's killers in a special defence of incrimination lodged at Ferris's trial.

7

THE DISAPPOINTMENT

WHILE I HAD my hands full in London, key witnesses in Ferris's trial were losing their bottle. They were claiming they were terrified by threats they had received as a result of their decision to testify and the inquiry team were worried they would fold. David Logue, Willie Gillen and wee Barney were already in safe houses with alarms that enabled them to summon the police at any hour of the night or day. But now it was decided it would be better to move them round the country, keeping their identities hidden and providing them with 24-hour cover.

I had met David Logue several times earlier in the inquiry and we got along well because I had been able to speak to him at his level, without talking down to him. So when he heard he was getting a permanent guard, he asked for me by name. This was in the early days of witness protection. No formal training or advice was given as to how we would care for the needs of the witnesses, in respect of their safety, their welfare and their families' welfare. We used our own initiative when choosing where to stay and when to move on prior to the court case. We were thrown in at the deep end and told to get on with it. We simply made it up as we went along, trying our best to be sympathetic to the witnesses, as well as playing along with the needs of the police service, or should I say senior management within the police, who at this time were naive about what was required. I was game to give it a go, although I had no idea how demanding a task it was going to be to keep such loose cannons in our control. At first, I was asked if I would mind going back and regaining my firearms certificate so I could give David armed protection. But when he realised that if I carried a gun we would not be able to go into the pubs and clubs, he decided he would prefer us to be unarmed.

Four of us were allocated to 'mind' David, with at least two officers on duty at any one time. I was still working in tandem with an officer called Mike. Every so often, we would all meet up in London Road police station, pick a new town and take a bundle of notes to cover our expenses. Our cover story was that we were painters and decorators, doing a major job away from home and that we were staying in bed and breakfasts to save us travelling back and forth every night. The first place we stayed was a guesthouse in Dumbarton, up on the Clyde coast. We told the owner we were doing a job at Faslane, the nearby submarine base. When the other officers came on duty, they told her they were part of the same team and that we were having a few days with our families. She seemed to accept this readily enough, glad, I guess, just to have customers so early in the year.

Logue had a history of petty thieving, so the first problem for us was trying to ensure he kept on the right side of the law while under witness protection. We would go into a shop with him while he bought cigarettes and he would come out, his pockets bulging with chocolate, ice cream or newspapers. Then there was his girlfriend. Although he was the kind of unsettled character who didn't mind drifting around the country like tumbleweed, he did demand to be allowed out to see her without a chaperone from time to time. At first these snatched trysts were unofficial; but eventually we decided we had better tell the management in case we got ourselves into trouble.

The management were really good about the situation and suggested we take the couple away to a posh hotel in Aberfoyle for a couple of days' break. It wasn't exactly a win on the lottery – more a dirty weekend courtesy of the police with two detectives playing gooseberry – but it was better than a night in front of the television. In the end, the somewhat bizarre arrangement lent some light relief to an operation that was, quite often, extremely tense. It is difficult to imagine what the hotel's traditional clientele dressed in their 'country casuals' cardigans made of our group of three men and one woman, particularly when David came down for the Saturday night dinner dance in a shell-suit and trainers, while his girlfriend wore leggings and a low-cut blouse. Indeed the whole meal degenerated into a farce: David's girlfriend continually complained, firstly because she didn't realise a salmon cut was fish and then because the menu offered sautéed potatoes and she wanted chips.

Back at the bed and breakfast, David's rough and ready background was equally difficult to hide. Try as we might to get him to tone down his behaviour, obscene language would rush out of his mouth before he could stop it. One morning, the landlady, Margaret, asked him if he would like some fresh orange juice with his breakfast. 'No, it runs the shite out me,' he replied, to our embarrassment. But Margaret was great. She said: 'Aye, it does that to me as well.' That broke the ice and we just collapsed laughing.

From there, we moved to a hotel down in Largs – a seaside town famous for its Italian ice cream – where David again proved difficult to rein in. He used to sneak into the manager's office, make himself at home behind his big oak desk and call his girlfriend. The manager would come back and catch him at it and David would just get up and walk out without a word of apology, as if all the guests carried on long conversations from his private telephone. At times, the whole thing became rather wearing and we began to wonder what kind of job we had got ourselves into. The lowest point was probably when we all got thrown out of Stirling swimming baths because David and his girlfriend were splashing and fighting in the water.

In quiet moments, David used to regale us with tales of his exploits on the streets. He said he was such an efficient car thief, his 'clients' had issued him with a pager so they could place an order with him at any time of the day. For example, if a particular taxi company had a 2.3 Sierra Diesel whose engine had seized, they would page him with all its details and he would steal a vehicle of the same year and model and drive it to their garage. The engine of the stolen car would be taken out and placed in the taxi and the stolen car would be towed away and dumped. It would all be done so discreetly, the taxi driver wouldn't be aware he had been given a stolen engine. I still to this day wonder what my life would have been like if I had continued running around with the Gorbals' car thieves.

The company that David had kept made him an asset on occasions. Out in the car with Mike one day, David suddenly shouted, 'Stop'. Pointing to a man hanging around a street corner, he said: 'He's keeping edgy', which translates as, 'He is acting as a lookout for a team of criminals.' Sure enough, minutes later, a second man came out of a close to join him. Mike called out officers from the division and they found the thief's pockets stuffed with jewellery. The police got a result and David earned himself £50 for the tip-off. But good days like that would be followed by incidents that reminded you of his bad side. Once, almost forgetting who we were, he told us how it amused him to think the car he had stolen could have been used in the murder and how he laughed even more heartily when he discovered the vehicle had previously belonged to a police inspector.

While we were finding life with David eventful, the teams watching Gillen and wee Barney were having an impossible time. Wee Barney was still on drugs and every time he met up with members of his family, they would supply him with gear and he would go off and snort it or inject it in the toilets. He could not resist the temptation to steal and was lifting stuff wherever he was taken. On a single trip to the ten-pin bowling, two purses went missing. The officers involved couldn't do anything about it because they couldn't blow their cover.

As for the four uniformed officers guarding Gillen, they appeared to have lost the plot. The main priority was to keep everyone's tempers in check, to humour the witnesses until we got them safely into court. But Gillen was throwing tantrums and, instead of indulging him like a spoilt child, the officers were hitting back and threatening to arrest him. The officers' nerves were frayed by a stressful job that seemed to go on and on.

The high tension was not relieved by the start of the trial, as we were all aware of how fragile the prosecution's case was. The police's reputation was on the line because the eyes of the country were on Glasgow High Court.

Security was high, with armed officers on guard, and the press benches were always full of reporters. But from the very first day, things went badly for the police. Witnesses kept changing their stories and their credibility was ripped to shreds the moment they were cross-examined.

Ferris, however, played his cards perfectly. He dressed in a sharp suit and got into the habit of saying 'Good morning' to the jury. So friendly was he towards the 15 in whose hands his destiny lay that the judge, Lord McCluskey, had to warn one female juror to stop smiling at him.

The lowest point in the trial was reached when supergrass Dennis Woodman took the stand for five days. He had been in Barlinnie when Ferris was remanded on the kneecapping charge and was supposed to be the linchpin in the prosecution's case. Woodman testified that Ferris had confessed his involvement in Arthur junior's murder to him while in jail, but the way he behaved in court did him no favours. The judge, Lord McCluskey, let Woodman's outbursts of anger go unchecked, explaining later that he had allowed him to act as he did to demonstrate to the jury what kind of person he was. Later Woodman's estranged wife told the court she was divorcing him because he 'told that many lies'.

Throughout the trial, everyone was on edge. Understandably, as the day approached where he was to take the stand, David Logue was getting increasingly hyper. He would read the court reports from the previous day's newspapers and laugh. He laughed the hardest when he found out Arthur senior had described him as 'the scum of the earth', but there was a manic edge to his voice that made us increasingly uneasy. On the one hand, he was plainly terrified at the prospect of giving evidence against Ferris, but, on the other, he was a megalomaniac who enjoyed the measure of celebrity his part in the trial afforded him. He revelled in the attention he attracted from other officers when we were forced to take him inside police stations, where he would listen intently to the radio messages in the hope of gaining any useful titbits of information.

On 20 April, we received a telephone call warning us that David would be called the next day. We were under instructions not to tell him, but he wasn't stupid and soon picked up on our excitement. The result was that we sat up all night in a hotel off Great Western Road going through his evidence over and over again at his request. We were not coaching him, just trying to reassure him about the difficult task that lay ahead. In an attempt to calm his nerves we reminded him that Strathclyde Police said they would take care of him and make sure he was safe and financially secure. The understanding was that he would have 24-hour protection at least until the end of the trial. He believed he had also been promised a new identity and a new home where he could live a better life in relative obscurity.

The following morning, we feted David like a hero and in a strange way he really was courageous. Although he was a prolific car thief, he was prepared to risk everything he had to cut himself off from everyone he knew in the underworld in order to take the stand. We had bought him a smart outfit to give him some credibility in the witness box and, by now close to nervous wrecks, we headed for the court in an unmarked car and smuggled him in through the side door. Legal arguments and the usual court delays meant there were more tense moments as we paced up and down, waiting for the final call.

When David finally stepped into the witness box, he was shaking with fear, but he gave it his best shot. He told his story, exactly as he had done before: how Ferris had asked him to steal a car, how he had spotted the Nissan Bluebird at East Kilbride station, realised it belonged to a commuter who would be away all day, and stole it. He went on to tell the jury how he later heard Arthur junior had been murdered and realised the car he had stolen had been used in the job.

But the cross-examination went really badly, with allegations we hadn't expected to come out used to undermine David's credibility. One of Scotland's top defence advocates, Donald Findlay, who was representing Ferris, asked David how the scar on his face had been caused. David said Ferris had slashed him because he believed he had broken into the home of one of Ferris's friends. David categorically denied being responsible – and indeed I don't believe he was a burglar. But the damage had been done. Findlay had successfully cast doubt on David's credibility by suggesting not only that he was a crook, but that he had a grudge against Ferris that might lead to him giving false testimony against him in court.

This was a great disappointment to the force as so much had been riding on David's testimony, but Mike and I both felt he had kept his side of the bargain and we were proud of our achievement. We had got him to the court in one piece and without falling out with him, which at times had been very, very difficult. As he was still on a high, we took him back to the police station – where he was thanked by senior officers – and then out for an expensive meal with plenty to drink to follow, before returning late at night to the hotel.

At 8.30 the following morning my mobile rang and I was told I was needed in Easterhouse on another murder inquiry. At first, my head was so fuzzy, the news didn't sink in. But then I realised that I was being asked to dump David the second he was no longer required. Worse still, they were leaving it to me to break the news.

As soon as I left for the Easterhouse murder, David stormed into London Road, shouting the odds. He was livid about the way he had been treated and was threatening to go straight to the newspapers if something wasn't done about it immediately. Eight hours later, I was back on witness protection, but it was clear the financial package David had anticipated was not going to be forthcoming and it was left to Mike and myself to sort out his relocation. Ferris had been acquitted. With Strathclyde police suffering a major humiliation, David's fate was the last thing on their minds. He had served his purpose and now the force could not care less what happened to him. He believed he had been let down and Mike and I felt guilty about that so, despite the fact it was no longer our responsibility, we tried to help him as best we could.

David insisted he wanted to remain in Glasgow despite everything that had happened, so we helped him find a flat to rent and fitted it with a panic button just to be on the safe side. For the first few months David had my phone number and we were in almost constant touch. He would know exactly where to find me, even on my days off, if he needed anything.

Gradually, he began to re-establish himself in the criminal fraternity and, for a while, he was a good informant. But eventually he was in so deep I was forced to take a step back. He would leave stolen goods lying around when I went to visit. If I had stayed around any longer, I would have been crossing a line. Of course, I didn't turn David in, I just began to keep my distance. It wasn't easy, though, because David had become used to the set-up and didn't really want to let go. He started to complain that he was being threatened again. This time, I think, he was just attention-seeking, but I arranged for another move, this time to Earl Street in Scotstoun, and he took with him a new girlfriend who he eventually married. After this, I cut my ties completely. Eventually David, who had begun to dabble in drugs, was charged after the drugs squad found a kilo of amphetamines in his flat. It was mostly his own fault, of course, but David was bitter because he believed if he had been treated properly he could have adopted a completely new lifestyle and would not have drifted back into crime. Instead he was dumped in another scummy flat and left to get on with it.

There were a lot of lessons learned during this, the first witness protection scheme. Strathclyde now have in place a team of well-trained and experienced officers dedicated to the Witness Protection Scheme, with guidelines and procedures firmly in place to assure and protect the future of the witness irrespective of the trial outcome.

The whole Ferris affair left a bad taste in the mouth of all the officers involved. Even before the trial, Ferris had been a familiar figure, but his high-profile acquittal on all charges, including the murder of Arthur Thompson junior and the kneecapping of Willie Gillen, won him the kind of celebrity normally reserved for football players. From the moment he stepped foot outside the court, his arms raised in triumph, he was famous and he lost no time in capitalising on his status. In the months that followed, he gave interviews to any newspaper that asked, and even agreed to take part in a documentary about his life. I'm sure he would argue this was the only way of clearing his name, but it seemed to the police as if he was mocking them for their failure.

He continued to play a leading role in the underworld, his hard-man reputation boosted by the publicity. He was sentenced to ten years in prison for gun-running offences in England and during his time in prison it was said that he continued to run his empire from within. Ferris is now a free man, serving only part of his original sentence. To our frustration, no one was ever charged with the murders of Hanlon and Glover. Arthur Thompson senior, who had lived so violently, and had survived several botched attempts on his own life, died naturally of a heart attack in 1995, opening the city up to a whole new power struggle.

8

THE ELITE

DISTRESSED THOUGH I was at everything that had happened during the Ferris affair, I had little time to fret about it because my career was moving so quickly. After the trial was over, I spent six months in Easterhouse CID before being chosen for the Scottish Crime Squad, an elite band of officers, hand-picked from all the forces in the country, to tackle the most serious offences, using the most advanced techniques and equipment. I joined the Scottish Crime Squad in 1993.

The Scottish Crime Squad's approach to policing was entirely different to anything I had experienced in my 16 years' service. Whereas in CID you tend to flaunt your position of authority to get results, in the crime squad, the emphasis is on secrecy. Most of the operations it carries out are covert. No one is supposed to find out what you are up to, not even your fellow officers in other divisions; that is your trump card, the element of surprise. This meant there was an entirely new jargon for me to learn, a language invented to enable crime squad officers to communicate on undercover operations. My love of intrigue and addiction to danger made this a very exciting prospect for me. The idea of secret stakeouts and dramatic drugs busts appealed to me in a sort of Boy's Own kind of way and I knew it was work I was suited to.

The first training course I went on taught me how to carry out surveillance from inside a Scottish Crime Squad vehicle. For three weeks, we were based down the west coast at Ayr, but we travelled the length and breadth of Scotland, covering 400 miles some days. We learned how to follow pedestrians in a car without attracting their attention and how to keep on their tail even if they suddenly head off through an alleyway inaccessible to cars. My particular forte, however, was high-speed driving. When I was working with the crime squad there were virtually no rules. Everyone drove high-performance cars. Accelerating to speeds of more than 100 mph, ignoring red lights, cutting other vehicles up at roadworks, were all par for the course, although this has since changed. I soon learned that if you are driving up a country lane and move out to overtake, the vehicle coming in the other direction from you will always brake to avoid hitting you. It took a lot of bottle, but as time went on I gained in confidence and knew the risks I was taking were calculated risks.

I was also asked if I wanted to go on an advanced motorcycle course within Strathclyde's traffic department. It was a chance I leapt at because, although I loved bikes when I was younger, I hadn't been on one for a long time. Motorcycles were crucial for long-distance surveillance because they could cut through heavy traffic and keep behind the target vehicle until the rest of the convoy caught up. I passed the first part of the course, which involved a 125 cc bike, with ease and quickly moved on to an 850 cc BMW model, which was a joy to ride. However, there was a down side to the course: because you were with the traffic department, you had to wear a uniform of a big yellow jacket and a police helmet. The motorcycle you rode on was also marked, something I was no longer used to. Needless to say, I soon got myself into trouble. I was riding into Balloch, on the edge of Loch Lomond, with my instructor, when two neds stuck their fingers up at us. Forgetting for a moment that they would know I was a police officer, I returned the gesture, and then rocked with laughter at the look of astonishment on their faces. But the traffic men didn't see the funny side. At that point, I knew I had done the right thing to come out of uniform and away from the humourless faces that often populated those departments and I promised myself I would never go back.

Despite my controversial behaviour, I passed the course and went back to the crime squad where I was given a 1100 cc. Every spare minute I had I spent practising on my bike, building up my confidence and my speed so I would be ready for anything.

The first big job I did on the bike involved a man from Cumbernauld who was smuggling drugs in from the continent via a 'private ambulance'. In fact the scam involved two identical vehicles – a 'clean' one, which he would drive out of this country, and a second one hidden at his destination with cannabis already sealed in its chassis. When he got there, he would simply swap vehicles, and take an accomplice on board to play the patient. Thus the drugs would be smuggled safely into Britain.

Our informer had told us the smuggler was due to travel to Spain to pick up a 'casualty' and drive back via Portsmouth with the drugs hidden inside. We followed him down to Portsmouth in a howling gale. It took nine hours, but we trailed him all the way to the ferry. Another team sailed across in the ferry with him, while a third was on stand-by in Bilbao to take over as he stepped on to dry land. My team was told to stay in Portsmouth so we were in place to tail him on his way back to Scotland the following day. There were 10 of us altogether, and, with more than 24 hours' free time in a town that was new to us, we went looking for a piece of the action. By lunchtime, we had found a pub that was doing a Budweiser promotion: drink six bottles and win a T-shirt. So we took bets on how many T-shirts we could take home with us and began a drinking marathon. We had already consumed a large amount of alcohol when our pagers started to go mad and we realised there must have been a change in plan.

We had been led to believe the drugs smuggler would travel to a town in Spain and change vehicles there. Instead, the registration plates were swapped just outside the ferry terminal so the second ambulance was able to board straight away. The drugs consignment was already on its way back to Britain and we were not fit to drive. We were as alarmed as you can be when you are seeing two of everything. After some garbled debate, we decided the best course of action was to go back to our hotels, to take long showers and try to grab a couple of hours' sleep.

By 6.15 p.m., we were back in the local police station being briefed, but we were still feeling under the weather. We decided that, since it was unlikely the ambulance would be doing more than 70 mph, we would probably be able to drive. But the journey proved to be more difficult than anticipated. For a start, instead of travelling north as we had expected, the driver headed first for London where he unloaded half the drugs into a lock-up. So, where it had taken nine hours to get down, it took us 12 to get back. I was soaked to the skin and I was dehydrated, but there wasn't any time to stop for a drink to quench my thirst. The most frightening thing was I could only go 180 to 200 miles on a full tank of petrol, so several times during the journey I had to refuel and then travel at speeds of up to 140 mph to catch up with the convoy. But, it was worth all the effort because when we arrived in Cumbernauld, we seized the ambulance and found 25 kilos still stashed inside. The other 25 kilos were recovered in London. The squad had a good result and we were all of us exhausted, but we were happy with our achievement.

The next course I went on focused on rural surveillance and was taught by, among others, an ex-member of the SAS. It involved lying in ditches and wide-open fields for hours on end without being spotted in order to keep watch on targets in inaccessible, rural sites. This was one of the most demanding parts of the training as it tested your stamina and your focus. Dressed in camouflage gear, with a Gore-Tex jacket as protection against the cold winter nights, you would position yourself beside a hedge or in a small trench, sometimes walking a mile and a half across country to get there. SAS-style radios would be attached to your ears and, for hours on end, your attention would be fixed on the target or the location at which you expected the crime to take place. The only food you would carry would be Mars Bars to keep your sugar levels up. One night, I spent 12 hours outside a hotel in Dumfries and Galloway with another officer in sub-zero temperatures. It was so cold that, every 25 minutes, one of us had to roll over to a spot where we couldn't be seen and do 50 press-ups in order to get the blood flowing again. We had been told the hotel was going to be targeted by a team of armed robbers but it eventually became apparent we had been given a false steer.

Not long after I got back from the course, there was an armed robbery on a post office in East Kilbride. The getaway vehicle had been last seen driving along back roads towards a village called Jackton and the Scottish Crime Squad was called in to try to establish if any evidence had been disposed of along the route. Eventually, on the road to Jackton, the officers discovered a holdall, containing a shotgun and balaclavas, tucked in behind a hedge, just waiting for someone to come along and pick it up. We replaced the holdall with an identical bag and then dug trenches about 15 ft away at a spot that gave us a clear view of the hedge. Other crime squad cars were positioned all along the back roads, ready to move in as soon as we gave the word. We were in constant communication with them through our radios. Wearing our camouflage gear and clutching our night-sights, we psyched ourselves up for a long night. By about 11 p.m., it was pitch black and very, very still. Suddenly, a car appeared from nowhere and drove past the site, slowing down as it did so. Minutes later, the same vehicle returned, moving even more slowly than before, and a figure jumped out. As the man headed for the bag, we whispered, 'Strike, strike, strike,' into our radios. The man ran back from the site and jumped into the still-moving vehicle, but just as the door closed, all the crime squad cars in the East Kilbride area converged on the site and came screeching to a halt. The occupants in the car were busted and we had another good result.

I was also involved in busting a pair of thieves who lived behind a service station near to Edinburgh. Their specialty was breaking into pubs and clubs after hours and raiding the fruit machines, but it was difficult for us to monitor activity at their houses because they were surveillance-conscious and lived in quiet streets where the presence of unaccustomed vehicles would have been very conspicuous.

To get round the problem, another officer and myself were told to position ourselves on rural land between the service station and the houses and to keep watch on them from there. And the very first night we staked them out, we struck lucky. It wasn't long before a car carrying the first suspect drew up at the second suspect's house and the second suspect jumped in. The pair of burglars then drove towards Dundee, with crime squad cars in hot pursuit.

At about 2 a.m., they turned into the drive of a large hotel near the Forth Road Bridge. They forced their way into the building, but by the time they emerged with their loot they were completely surrounded. The drivers of the crime squad cars watched in wry amusement as the thieves came out pushing a plastic bin stuffed full of drink and the fruit machine takings. They were caught red-handed and were charged, not only with the break-in at the pub, but also with a succession of burglaries they had previously committed in the area.

The boys in the squad, or the 'squaddies' as we were sometimes affectionately called, had a warped but amusing sense of humour. One of my detective inspectors – of whom I was very fond and had previously served with – was a charismatic man who liked a good joke. Ron Gallahan had early in his service suffered the loss of a finger while chasing a ned. Ron had jumped a fence, catching the ring he wore on a rusty nail and leaving his finger behind. When conducting his briefings in the squad he would express himself with the use of his hands and it was hypnotic to watch, your gaze concentrating on the missing finger.

I remember when Ron's time in the squad was finished and he was returning to division. The team had collected money to buy him a going-away present, as was the norm. Russell – my old partner from division – and I asked Ron what he wanted. Ron said he would like a matching pen and pencil set. By arrangement Ron went on his own to the Argyle Arcade in Glasgow to choose what he wanted. The arcade houses some of the finest jewellery shops in Scotland. The following day Russell and I were dispatched to collect Ron's pre-selected gift. The woman behind the counter seemed like a relative of Her Majesty the Queen and spoke as if she had a mouth full of marbles. Her Majesty showed Russell and I the present, which was housed in a beautiful velvet presentation box. We both looked at each other and laughed – evidently on the same wavelength – and asked her if she would supply us with an empty presentation box. When we explained our reasons she almost fainted. Prior to returning to the office Russell and I made an unscheduled stop at a local party shop.

The present was gift-wrapped and given to the Commander of the squad to present to Ron later that day at the same time as giving a small speech thanking Ron for his services during his time in the squad. By the time 5 p.m. came we all had had a few beers and the jokes were flying. The bosses were in the Commander's room having a small dram. At 5.30 p.m. the Commander and his understudies came into the crew room to make the presentation. The Commander made his speech, which was justified. He then handed over the gift-wrapped set. Ron accepted his gift and placed it in front of him. Russell and I began to heckle, telling him to open the gift. Ron refused, explaining that everyone in the room knew what it was. We pushed the issue and Ron conceded. Taking time not to rip the gift paper, Ron eventually opened the velvet box, at the same time turning to show the Commander its contents. When the Commander saw the contents he went bright red and Ron, being a perceptive individual, glanced down at the case to see a plastic finger covered in artificial blood sitting proudly where the pen and pencil should have been. Ron burst out laughing and shared the joke with the onlookers. The wind-up went down well.

Ron's reply to the Commander's speech has remained with me. Ron took us back to our younger days in the job saying, 'I remember when the old cops moaned about the job being fucked, or as we all know, the abbreviated version, "TJF". How many times have we all heard that said?' Ron continued. 'I have my own thoughts and feelings about that well-used phrase. As long as I have got good guys like you' – he pointed to the gathered ensemble – 'around me, those words will never pass my lips. The job is not fucked.' Ron was right: as long as I was working with a good bunch of guys then the words would never pass my lips and so far in my police service that day had not yet arrived.

I had been involved in a succession of successful operations when I was first approached about the possibility of becoming an undercover. I knew I was addicted to danger, yet life as an undercover was not something I had really thought about. Although I knew such work existed, the operations of the undercovers were shrouded in secrecy; no one ever knew what they were up to.

I was immediately taken with the idea as I could see I was suited to it, but, by this time, I was married to Wendy and was worried about how she would react to the dramatic change in lifestyle. The nature of the work meant she would be isolated for weeks, sometimes months at a time, often unable to get in touch with me. I knew she would worry about me as I mixed with some of the most dangerous men in Britain and that this would place an enormous strain on her. But Wendy, a former special branch officer, is no stranger to stress and has always supported me in everything I have wanted to do. When she realised how much I wanted to give it a try, she said, 'Go for it' and I did.

However, just because you have been approached about the possibility of undercover work there is no guarantee you will be accepted for it and I still had a long way to go. A succession of hurdles in the shape of gruelling interviews and psychometric tests have to be overcome before you are deemed suitable material for a job that will push you to your limits. After initial interviews at the Scottish Crime Squad, I was chosen, along with three other officers, to go down to Scotland Yard for the final round of the selection process. In the morning, we had to answer 700 questions aimed at assessing our character and inner resources. This session drained me of all self-confidence. I did my best, but I had no idea if I had given the answers they required and I began to doubt I had the appropriate qualities.

The following day, however, at a rigorous interview conducted by a superintendent from special branch, I felt I had fared better. The interview panel consisted of the Superintendent, a psychologist and a divisional commander. During the interview I was asked if would I tell my wife the full details of an undercover job I was on, bearing in mind the secrecy involved in this type of work. Much to the surprise of the panel I said I would tell her everything. I then realised by their reactions that I had hit a sore point.

They then began to badger and probe me with questions: 'What if your wife tells someone? What if you split up in later years? She would know all about the network of the undercover system.' They could not believe my answer. They looked at me hoping I would withdraw what I had said.

'No, I am sorry. I don't agree. I would tell her everything,' I said.

The Superintendent sat forward, moving in for the kill. 'Do you trust her. Can you be sure?'

I decided to have some fun. I led them up the garden path, giving them all the wrong answers to their questions about Wendy. Eventually the Commander sat forward and asked why was I so trusting in my wife, 'What does she do for a living?'

Bingo. They had walked right into it. Smugly I replied, 'She is an intelligence officer working with Special Branch.' The psychologist gave a smile and wrote down some comments on her pad. They obviously had not read my notes.

I had rehearsed this scenario so many times in my head and my efforts paid off. I was asked if at any stage in my career had I taken a calculated risk. I told them how, when carrying out surveillance on my motorbike, I often had to decide if it was safe to overtake the vehicle in front at 120 mph. I was asked how I would feel infiltrating a paedophile ring and I told him that, although it would be unpleasant and I wouldn't like it, I was prepared to do anything to prevent further child abuse. There were also questions aimed at establishing if I understood and could resist the temptations the job might lay before me. For example what would I do if I had to hang around with prostitutes? How would I cope with an operation that revolved around a pub? Would I be able to back off, without provoking suspicion, if I was offered drugs?

It was explained the reason for this grilling was that people who work undercover for a long period of time sometimes suffer from what is known as the Stockholm syndrome, where they begin to identify so closely with the communities they are infiltrating they lose sight of the operation. After a while it is no longer clear if they are police officers setting up drug deals to catch suppliers or part of the ring itself. The police service had to be sure the officers they picked were aware of this pitfall and were capable of avoiding it.

I answered all the questions as best I could, but still as I took the flight back home I was despondent. A week went by without any news, but then, to my relief I was called in and told I was one of two Scottish Crime Squad officers to have passed. From then on, my life was never to be the same again.

Within a couple of months, I was heading for a residential course that would teach me how to blend into an alien environment, to win the trust of criminals so you can pry into their lives without raising their suspicions. Being born in the Gorbals would certainly help me blend in.

Where on some courses you might be expected to bring a suitcase, we were told to come armed with a 'legend' – a fictional past that will accompany you throughout your time as an undercover. This is not as easy as it sounds. The undercover's legend must be detailed enough for him not to seem evasive, but vague enough to prevent suspicious criminals doing too much sniffing around. For this reason I looked to the Gorbals for inspiration. By this time, most of the buildings that I remembered from my childhood had been demolished so I could lay claim to 'old haunts', safe in the knowledge that if anyone ever decided to check up on me, they would find the premises I described had disappeared. To further protect myself from inquisitive minds, I decided my mother and father had long since died and that I managed to make it into my 30s without a criminal record. Although I was an armed robber and drug dealer, I had successfully evaded capture by the police, making me an ideal accomplice.

The two weeks I spent on the course were amongst the most intense of my life. Every day we worked from 7 a.m. to 11 p.m., learning the dos and don'ts of life as an undercover. On the first day, those who had spent years in this strange double life described their own experiences to their captive audience. They told us of the hazards they had encountered, the risks they had taken and the stress they had endured. They explained the need to keep your notebooks up to date throughout the operation and emphasised the importance of knowing the limits of your remit, of never getting involved in an illegal activity you couldn't justify in court.

After listening awestruck to the theory, we started to take part in a series of simulated operations. Suddenly aware that this was not a game, that at some stage my life might depend on what I had been taught on this course, my attention never wavered for a second.

In the first exercise, I was told I had to buy counterfeit money from a supplier. An initial meeting had been set up in a pub by another undercover who had told the target I wanted to take thousands of fake £20 notes off his hands. At this encounter, I had been told, I was to win the man's trust, to prove I was trustworthy and to lay the groundwork for a future deal.

Slightly nervous at the prospect of my first practical test, I arrived at the pub to be greeted by a cockney wide-boy with a gold a ring on every finger, who introduced himself as Ray. Almost immediately he started interrogating me about my past, so, almost immediately, I went on the defensive. Instinctively, I turned the tables on him and started accusing him of asking so many questions, he must be Old Bill. This is a technique often used by undercovers because it puts the target on the back foot. They are less likely to probe your background because they are too busy trying to prove their own criminal credentials. Eventually we agreed to do a 'test' deal where I purchased just a couple of £20 notes. I told Ray I would get the fake money checked out and, if it proved to be good quality, we would meet again for further negotiations.

The following morning, I phoned him to say I had decided to buy £50,000 of the notes from him and to arrange a meeting as soon as possible to complete the deal. I knew we would have to negotiate the actual handover because he would not trust me to honour my side of the bargain and vice versa, so we met in a pub to thrash out the details. Each of us came in a car driven by an 'accomplice' to help ensure everything went smoothly.

Over a meal it was decided that Ray and his man would get in my car to check the money, and then we would all move over to his car to check the notes. If everything was satisfactory, the drivers would exchange packages, while we stayed in the vehicles.

The operation seemed to be going well. But the minute we stepped outside the pub, Ray said he wanted to dust me down. I put up no objection because I wasn't wired – it had been decided earlier that it was simpler for the other undercover to record the transactions. Just as we were about to get into my car, I realised I should have searched him too. At first he objected, but then he changed his mind and allowed me to dust him down too. I checked him for wires and weapons. I noticed a bulge in his coat pocket, but he said it was his mobile phone and I accepted his reply.

He jumped into the front of my car as I climbed in the back. My man was still in the driver's seat. I showed Ray the money and he said, 'That's fine,' but as he did so, he reached into the coat pocket and pulled out a handgun. He put it to the driver's head and pulled the trigger, then turned it round and did the same to me, saying: 'You're both dead.' Then he walked away.

I couldn't believe I had made such a fundamental mistake. I had taken a criminal's word and hadn't physically checked that what he was telling me was true. If it had been a real job, there would have been two dead undercovers and the target would have walked off with £50,000. I headed back to base kicking myself for having been so stupid and walked in to find Ray sitting there with all the other officers. I was mortified, but he laughed and shook my hand. He knew I'd been given such a shock that I had learned my lesson.

The course leaders found lots of ingenious ways to demonstrate the need for some of the rules undercovers have to abide by. On one occasion, a female officer was told to choose from one of three local shops from which to buy a packet of condoms. If this wasn't embarrassing enough, she was to grill the shop assistant about the product and then relay all the information she had gathered to the rest of the team. A male officer was asked to carry out the same exercise, only he was to buy sanitary towels.

In the evening, they came back to tell us how they had got on. The woman, looking a little bashful, admitted that although she had bought the condoms, she had been too embarrassed to ask the man who served her anything about them. She had simply lifted her groceries and made a sharp exit. The man on the other hand boasted about how successful his mission to buy sanitary towels had been. He said he had told the shopkeeper they were for his daughter who had just started her first period and he wanted to make sure he was buying the right thing and that the shopkeeper had given him all the information he required. It all sounded very impressive.

But then the instructor stood up and with a flick of a remote control, footage of the woman officer in the shop appeared on screen. She had told us all the truth. She went in, bought a newspaper, some bread and the condoms, paid at the cash desk and walked out. Then it switched to the male undercover. He had bought a newspaper and the sanitary towels but had said nothing to the shopkeeper. Safe to say the male officer's bravado was short lived; the camera never lies.

The instructor said: 'This is to show you how important it is that you tell the truth to your fellow officers, who need accurate information on which to base their decisions.' Obviously, you have to lie to the criminals, but even then, the instructor said, it is important to stick rigidly to your legend and not to add extraneous details that might trip you up. You never know when your targets might check up on you and you don't want them to be able to unearth any discrepancy in your story. I didn't know it then, but I was to find out, only too soon, how much checking a target might be prepared to do and how your life could be threatened by it.

One undercover, who had been involved in breaking a paedophile ring in England, gave us a graphic insight into how distasteful the job could be. His mission had been to buy child sex videos from the ringleader in an attempt to incriminate him, a task that would inevitably involve viewing hardcore footage. When the ringleader turned up at the undercover's flat, he was as disgusting a specimen as you could imagine, with greasy, matted hair, thick glasses, a stained shirt and slip-on shoes. The police officer told him he had his television and video set up so he could check the 'quality' of the material he was about to buy. 'Fine,' said the pervert. 'You'll join me in a wank as we're watching, won't you?' Listening to this lecture, the trainees were just stunned into silence, trying to imagine what on earth we would say to get ourselves out of this embarrassing situation, without jeopardising the operation. 'Pretend you have a disease' was one suggestion. But the undercover said, 'If you want to decline, without offending the target, just reply: "I would, but I had one just before you came in."' Even contemplating this sort of scenario, and the viewing of sexual assaults on children, made my blood run cold. But if you want to stop the sale of such videos, then these are the lengths to which you sometimes have to go.

The most dramatic moment in the course came by virtue of an FBI agent. He had been involved in a sting to bust a crack dealer with an officer called Marty, who was wired up and sent into a house. The FBI agent told us he was now going to play us the tape of the operation unfolding.

The first thing we can hear is Marty on his way up the stairs, identifying who he is and what he's about to do. Then we hear him talking to the crackheads in the house. It's clear from the way the conversation is going that he has been dealing with them for some time and there is an element of trust there. But then the mood suddenly changes. An argument breaks out between two of the men and Marty intervenes, trying to calm everyone down. Then a gun is fired. We actually hear the sound of the bullet going into Marty's chest and him slumping helplessly to the ground. The rasping and gurgling noises seem to go on forever, but then there is a clamour as the police officers, who have been monitoring the operation from outside, try to batter down the front door. Then the voice of the FBI agent giving the lecture is heard screaming: 'For God's sake, hang in there, man. There's an ambulance on the way.' Then the gurgling sound stops. Marty is dead.

The FBI agent was choked up as he told us that every time he hears the tape he has a flashback to the killing. He said we must realise we are not fireproof just because we are police officers, that we are as vulnerable as anyone else who mixes in dangerous circles.

We all sat in stunned silence, thinking about our colleague, 2,000 miles across the Atlantic, and realised, once more, that this wasn't a game; we really could die a horrible death as a result of what we were about to do.

The FBI lecture marked a turning point. If you could confront Marty's death and not back out, then you were going all the way.

9

FIRST BLOOD

THE MIND GAMES started during the latter half of the course until gradually it began to feel as if we were engaged in all-out psychological warfare. In order to test our resilience, the instructors tried to disorientate us, to confuse our body clocks.

By now, we were being actively encouraged to socialise at night, so we started drinking until the early hours of the morning. The instructors would at first tell us to be ready to go out on the first exercise at 7 a.m., but would call later on, after large quantities of alcohol had been consumed, to say the plan had changed and the exercise had been brought forward to 5 a.m. So we would be going out to meet some potential psychopath with a hangover and only a couple of hours' sleep. In the morning, the instructor would say: 'We'll finish at 9 p.m. today and let you off early.' And you would experience a wave of relief as you imagined your head sinking into the pillow. But come 9 p.m. it would emerge that one of the most important people due to lecture later on in the course was being called away on urgent business the next day, and so would be speaking at 11 p.m. You would arrive on time and would be left hanging around until 1 a.m. when the speaker finally showed up. By this time you knew your stamina was being tested, but you were gasping for a drink to relieve the stress and so the sleep deprivation programme continued. At the same time, you had to keep your wits about you as you were under constant scrutiny from the instructors, who devised hair-raising scenarios to assess your attitude, loyalty and mental health and to point out the pitfalls that lay ahead.

One day, we were told one of the undercover officers on our course had been sent out to collect a mystery parcel from a man in an Underground station and to bring it back to the office. We were out on exercises all day and when they were finally over, we expected to see our fellow undercover back at headquarters, his mission complete. However, there was no sign of him and the rumour mill was going wild: he'd been sent home in disgrace; he'd had enough and walked out. But in fact the truth was much more alarming.

The officer, Matt, had gone to the Underground and taken possession of the parcel as directed. But less than 20 yards around the corner, he had been stopped by two uniformed officers, who had witnessed the handover and who believed a crime to have been committed. Matt was ordered to produce the parcel, which was then opened in front of him. To his horror, it contained two sticks of gelignite. Matt had been arrested under the Explosives Act and held at the local police station where he was held for six hours. Despite a rigorous interrogation, he kept rigidly to the undercover's code. He did not reveal his true identity in an attempt to make life easier for himself or give any details of the exercise on which he was engaged. It had been drilled into us that this was one rule we had to keep, even if we feared our silence would mean the case against us reached a courtroom. It was important because the identity of undercovers must be a closely guarded secret known only by a handful of trusted, senior officers.

Matt must have been terrified to be arrested for such a serious offence with no one there to bail him out, but he was one of the best officers on the course and he kept his nerve. In the end, it turned out his arrest was a set-up designed to show us how easy it would be to find yourself in this situation and how difficult it would be to deal with it, and it certainly achieved its aim. Once out in the real world, however, we were offered a measure of protection: the emergency contact number of a senior police officer or well-briefed solicitor we could phone in such an eventuality.

Equally ruthless was the kidnap and torture of one of the undercovers –

Ken – during a simulated drugs sting. Ken had met two guys in a house to discuss the setting up of a deal, but they apparently smelled a rat and the encounter turned nasty. They searched him and discovered his tape recorder, so, in a desperate attempt to convince them he wasn't a police officer, he told them he was an investigative journalist with the *News of the World*. At that, the men, who turned out to be members of the Specialist Boat Services, stripped Ken down to his underpants, handcuffed him and put him in a wardrobe. For six or seven hours he was kept in there and brought out occasionally to be beaten. The ordeal ended as he passed out in the wardrobe after a hood was placed over his head. At his debriefing, he was told his fatal flaw was not the decision to say he was an investigative journalist, a ruse which might have worked, but not checking his equipment. On the back of his tape machine was a label with the words 'Metropolitan Police' written on it. It was clear he had been lying to the drug dealers and he had to pay the price for his act of betrayal.

By the end of the course, any illusion that undercover work was either entertaining or glamorous had been shattered. It was clear that for the duration of your time as an undercover, you would give your entire life over to the job, and that you would be taking mind-boggling risks every single day.

One officer out of the 12 had already dropped out, and it was clear several more were struggling. But Gary and I, along with the London officers, had thrived under the pressure. As a result, I was asked if I would like to take up a three-month secondment with the Met, which was short of Scottish officers. I turned it down, however, because Wendy did not want me working so far away from home, in a city full of temptations.

Instead, Gary and I returned to Scotland to await our first assignment. It was not long coming and it was to prove just as demanding and as nerve-racking as I had anticipated.

Within five weeks, I was brought in to target a drug pusher operating in the North East of England – a slippery character called Ritchie who dealt in cocaine and had successfully evaded operations by Northumbria Police and the regional crime squad. A fellow undercover called Marianne had already had one successful meeting with Ritchie, who appeared to have taken a liking to her, and I was being asked to provide her with cover for the rest of the sting.

By the time I appeared on the scene, Marianne had already organised a second meeting with the target at a pub in Newcastle's city centre at which the possible purchase of a 'tester' was to be discussed. If the tester proved satisfactory, the story went, she would buy more to take back up to Scotland with her. She was to be the courier, the 'donkey', and later, I would be introduced as the money man behind the deal. That way, I could provide an element of protection and corroboration.

At this stage, however, my job was simply to run Marianne to the pub and to pick her up afterwards. She had a wire in her handbag and was supposed to keep Ritchie talking as long as possible to obtain plenty of incriminating material on tape. Even though it wasn't me whose life was on the line, my stomach was churning as I tried to think of everything that Marianne would need to remember in order to protect herself. As we travelled together in the car, it was as if we were actors preparing for a stage performance. I tried to help Marianne become her alter ego by rehearsing her lines with her over and over again.

She was gone for two tense hours during which time I could do nothing but watch the hands of the clock. When she emerged from the dimly lit bar, she waited until she was sure she was not being watched and then headed back to the car. As soon as she opened the door, I could see she was so high on excitement an outsider could mistakenly have believed she had been consuming the drugs she had been sent to buy. I had realised I might have to scrape her off the ceiling, but even so, I was taken aback by how difficult it was to debrief her. She was talking incessantly and much too fast, and her voice was five octaves higher than it had been; the meeting had gone better than expected. Ritchie clearly trusted her and was prepared to go through with the deal. Marianne was buzzing because she knew success was within her grasp. It was great to share her excitement and to realise that very soon I would be experiencing the same fantastic adrenaline rush.

When we got back to Morpeth, in Northumberland, where Crime Team North was based, our progress was scrutinised by the Detective Inspector leading the investigation. It was time for me to be introduced into the equation. But where, in normal circumstances, Marianne would have told her target in advance I would be turning up, it was decided we should take a different approach on this occasion. Ritchie was a particularly nervous character, extremely wary of strangers. So I was told to turn up cold at his next meeting with Marianne, so as to give him no chance to lose his nerve and back out of the deal.

The encounter was set up for 1 p.m. one day in the following week. In order to look the part of an established seller, I dressed in designer gear: a smart jacket, a casual polo-neck and expensive-looking shoes. We hired a Mercedes 180 and made our way to Newcastle, both excited by the prospect of the strike we thought was now inevitable. At 12.45 p.m., we were both ensconced, eating a bar lunch in order to avoid arousing suspicion. By 1.30 p.m., however, there was still no sign of Ritchie and Marianne was starting to get very fidgety. She phoned him. He apologised for being late but promised he would turn up at some point.

When he finally walked in with his runner, a man called Derek, he wasn't at all what I had expected. I had thought he would be quite a sophisticated criminal. But this man, who was the same height as me and in his early 30s, looked just like a labourer and I realised I had chosen entirely the wrong approach. It was immediately clear Ritchie was upset by my presence. He was visibly shaken by having to deal with an unknown quantity and by my apparent wealth, which made him feel uncomfortable. He felt I was somehow above him and I realised we were going to have to tread carefully if we were not to lose all the ground we had gained.

I went up to the bar to get the drinks in and to give Marianne a chance to reassure Ritchie I was kosher. Ritchie was a very excitable character with a strong Geordie accent and he spoke very, very fast, which made it difficult to understand him. On my return, I decided to steer a middle course; I would act neither as a hard man nor as a sophisticate but try to put myself over as a decent and ordinary guy. It seemed to work, because gradually he began to relax and even to apologise for his initial scepticism. Finally, after much chit-chat, we got around to discussing the deal. We told Ritchie that, if his prices were acceptable, we were prepared to buy 11 oz. of cocaine, but that we needed a sample to test the quality of the gear we were buying.

Ritchie agreed to give us a tester right away so Derek and I went off to the toilet where, without exchanging a word, he handed me a small package of powder for me to slip down the front of my trousers. When I got back to the table, I passed the package discreetly to Marianne, who put it in her bag. It was as simple as that. The first part of the deal was complete. We were parting company on reasonable terms. Although Ritchie was impressed by the Mercedes he had seen in the car park, he had clearly convinced himself I was a bigger fish than I had led him to believe. Ritchie and I shook hands and agreed not to contact each other for at least a week to give us a chance to get the drug tested, ostensibly by our people in Scotland, but in reality by Northumbria Police's forensic experts.

Back in the car, Marianne reached into her bag and switched off her tape and we exchanged smug glances, congratulating ourselves on some fast talking. We had both been justifiably wary about my turning up unannounced and the fact we managed to win Ritchie's confidence is testament to our nerves of steel. We were certain we had lured our victim into our trap.

The only nagging doubt I had did not concern Ritchie at all, it concerned Marianne. Even five hours after we had left the Newcastle pub, when we had been thoroughly debriefed at Morpeth and were driving back up to Scotland, she was incredibly high. Throughout the journey home, she continued to talk excitedly, going over and over the significance of every word that had been said in the pub and the thought passed through my mind: 'Is Marianne emotionally stable enough for this job?'

A mundane week passed back at the Scottish Crime Squad before I was told that Ritchie had left a message and tests had confirmed the cocaine was good quality so the Detective Inspector decided we should go ahead with the deal. Marianne and I got together to decide what we were prepared to pay per ounce and then called him back to set up a meeting in the usual pub in Newcastle where we would finalise the deal. When we got there, however, we encountered a setback because Ritchie had sent Derek to speak to us instead of turning up in person.

When something like this happens, it is important to remember you are supposed to be a gangster and to act accordingly. If you show the dealers too much respect it will not take them long to suspect you are a police officer. Only a police officer would be so desperate for a strike that he would allow a dealer to call the shots in this way. So as soon as I saw Derek was there alone, I let rip. I told him I hadn't travelled all the way from Scotland to deal with the monkey. I wanted the organ grinder and promised that I would turn tail and head straight back up north unless Ritchie was prepared to deal with me directly. Derek, who had only just finished a three-year stretch for shoplifting, immediately apologised and soon came back to tell us he had persuaded Ritchie to meet us later that night at another hostelry for what was to be, we were told, primarily a social occasion.

By now, we were beginning to get a bit concerned that Ritchie was trying to distance himself from the deal. We got ourselves dressed up and agreed to go along with the night out. We were offered surveillance, but turned it down, taking the Detective Inspector's home telephone number in case of emergencies. Since no deal was to be struck, we weren't even wired.

It quickly became clear Ritchie and Derek were expecting us to join them in a heavy drinking session. After a couple of pints in Scruffy Murphy's, they announced we would spend the rest of the night on a pub crawl before heading for a less than salubrious venue beneath the city's bus station. Once inside the seedy basement, Ritchie told me in a whisper to follow him into the toilets. I had absolutely no idea what he wanted from me. The worst possibilities were spinning round in my head. Has he found out I'm a police officer? Will he stuff me into one of the cubicles and then kick my head into a pulp? I knew Marianne was scared because I could see her gulping down her drink and my Adam's apple was going up and down like a yo-yo. But, I also knew they would be scrutinising our reactions and making judgments based upon them, so I tried to send out the right signals and hoped they wouldn't be able to tell I was rigid with fear.

I walked along the corridor like a condemned man, resigned to my fate. Ritchie and Derek disappeared into a cubicle and then called me in. I pushed open the door with trembling hands to find they had set up three lines of coke on the cistern and were snorting it through a five-pound note. 'Come on,' they said. 'Take some charlie with us.'

One of the most important rules of being an undercover is that, even under extreme pressure, you must refuse any offer of drugs. Failure to do so is considered gross misconduct and will result in instant dismissal. This may sound obvious, but, if you have infiltrated a community in which everyone is a user, saying no to a roll-up, a line or a hit can make you very conspicuous indeed. This was the first time I had been faced with this dilemma, but I stuck to the line I had been taught on the course. 'No way. I sell the fuckin' stuff but I don't use it. That's why I have money in my pocket and a Mercedes in the garage.' I told Ritchie that if he wanted me to get high, he should buy me a malt whisky. He laughed. Only then did I know I was going to survive the night.

No sooner had one hurdle been overcome, however, than another came up to meet me. Back in the bar, Derek vanished before reappearing at our table with two tarty-looking women. The first was introduced as his wife, but the second, an attractive blonde with a small skirt and large cleavage, had no obvious partner. As the evening wore on, she flirted and edged closer and closer. As she confided that her husband was in the army and she hadn't seen him for more than six months, the conclusion was unavoidable: this woman was being laid on for me as part of the entertainment. Derek intimated to me that I should get rid of Marianne so the four of us could go on to a house party together. This was something for which we had no contingency plan. I didn't want to offend Ritchie, but I couldn't get involved with this woman and anyway, I needed Marianne with me as corroboration. Finally, I managed to grab a quick word with Marianne at the bar. I suggested that as a last resort we should tell them we had been seeing each other on and off for years, but that we didn't really want anyone to know about our relationship. So, as the woman became more and more obvious in her attentions, stroking my thigh and nibbling my ears, Marianne pretended to flounce off in a huff to the toilets. This was my cue to lean over to Derek and tell him discreetly that, much as I liked the woman they had laid on for me, Marianne and I were an item and it would be inappropriate to become involved with someone else while she was around. Derek apologised profusely for embarrassing me and everything seemed to be back on an even keel.

We continued drinking in an endless stream of the tacky bars Newcastle's Bigg Market is famous for and the deal was set up for the following morning. All we had to do was to phone Ritchie to set up a venue. In a pub where the bar staff dressed only in swimsuits and the music thumped out of the speakers so loudly we could have revealed our true identities and got away with it, we made our excuses and left for our hotel.

In the morning we drove straight to Morpeth to tell the team everything was set up. The DI had already put one surveillance team on Ritchie's house and another one on Derek's. We thought we would have everybody locked up by lunchtime, but it was not to be. When we phoned Ritchie there was no reply, but Derek said we should head to his house just outside Newcastle and pick him up and he would sort everything out. He emerged carrying a brown paper bag that he said contained clothes he was returning and made us drive him to the city centre and drop him off so he could 'finalise' arrangements.

Half an hour later, we tried his mobile again and he told us he had encountered a problem: the man who was guarding the gear had gone out to work and they couldn't get hold of him until 11 a.m. Another phone call, and the deal was being postponed until teatime. Things were looking very iffy now from our point of view. We had tried to go along with their instructions in order not to jeopardise the deal but it looked as though all our efforts had been in vain. I was beginning to wonder if Ritchie was even capable of laying his hands on 11 oz. of cocaine.

We decided it was time to up the ante. I started to take a very heavy approach with Derek. I told him I thought we were dealing with halfwits. 'I've got good money here and I want to buy the drugs but I'm not sitting here until 5 p.m., so you two arseholes better get the finger out,' I said. I told them the drugs were for a band that were playing in Glasgow that night and if I didn't have the gear for 2 p.m., then I was going straight back up north.

Come 2 p.m., we still hadn't heard anything and we felt we were being led a merry dance. We decided we should call it a day, so the DI stood down all the surveillance and we set off back up the A1. We were about four miles from Morpeth when the phone rang and it was Ritchie saying he had managed to get hold of the gear at last. Since the operation had been stood down, we had to think fast, but we decided to go for it. We told him to meet us at the Holiday Inn just outside Newcastle in an hour and a half, giving us just enough time to set up the surveillance again.

The team swung straight back into action. We booked a room overlooking the car park, where two vans full of officers from the Tactical Support Unit were parked so officers could monitor what was going on. We were to sit in the foyer surrounded by officers wearing covert radios. When Ritchie and Derek arrived we were to ask to see the drugs and then walk with them to the Mercedes, on the pretext of collecting the cash. As we left the hotel, I was to put on a pair of sunglasses if they were carrying the drugs. The moment the signal was given, the Tactical Support Unit would move in and arrest all three of us before we got anywhere near the car.

Everything was set up. Marianne and I were very tense as we sat drinking a steady stream of coffees in the hotel foyer. Five o'clock came and went and the tension was mounting. Suddenly a taxi drew up and there was Derek, clutching the same brown paper bag he had with him in the morning and looking very nervous. Clearly he had been carrying the drugs from early in the morning. For some reason, he and Ritchie, who had not turned up, had spent the day coming up with ways to stall us. Derek shook my hand and asked to see the money. I told him we were not doing business in the hotel bedroom but that we would have a look at the drug in the toilets. Marianne took the powder into the toilet, tested it and then gave the go-ahead.

As we left the hotel, I put on my sunglasses as planned. I felt sure I was seen as I was passing the first of three observation points and could see one of the officers looking out of the window. It was 200 yards to the car, the longest 200 yards I have ever walked in my life. Every second I expected the police cars to stop us in our tracks, but nothing happened. Marianne and I were trying to make small talk to ease the tension. I told Ritchie I was an armed robber back in Scotland and he replied: 'Och, we knew you weren't really a businessman.' About 25 yards from the Mercedes, we passed an unmarked blue Ford Transit van and there was a sudden clunk – the kind of noise you get if an officer drops his radio or his baton. All of us heard it quite clearly. After an eerie pause, Derek asked: 'What was that?'

I said it must be the heat expanding the roof and everyone agreed vociferously, but there was a change in Derek's face that betrayed his suspicions.

We were getting closer and closer to the car, but we knew if we were forced to get inside the game was up because there was no money in the vehicle – it was just for show. Robbie, my colleague from the course who was sitting in the driver's seat, knew we were never supposed to reach it, but there was nothing he could do. Marianne and I were getting desperate, but we were now alongside the Mercedes so we had no other choice but to open the doors.

I told Derek to get in the car, but, by now, he knew there was something wrong and he said: 'I'm not getting into any fucking car.' The next few minutes happened in slow motion. Marianne got into the back seat and I leaned over from the front passenger's seat to give her the drugs. The two of us were looking pleadingly at the blue van, when its doors flew open and six or seven officers ran towards us. Derek shouted out: 'You bastard. You've set me up. You're dead,' before starting to run. Throughout our training we had been told not to react; to keep playing the part of the criminal and to get arrested with everyone else. But at this point instinct took over and I grabbed him and threw him to the ground. Seconds later, the other officers arrived and we were all handcuffed and taken away in separate cars.

After it was all over, we went off to the pub with the officers who had been carrying out the surveillance. They told us they hadn't thought we would pull it off because we were getting the run around from Derek and Ritchie and I understood what they meant. When you are spending hour after hour on a stakeout and nothing appears to be happening it can be very demoralising, particularly if you are not being told why the operation isn't going as planned. When the officers were told to go to the Holiday Inn, they just thought it was more of the same so they weren't really mentally geared up for a result. But that couldn't explain why no one had moved in to make the arrests until we were in the car. As usual everyone blamed everyone else. The officers in the van had expected the strike to be called by the officers at the first window, who watched as I put my sunglasses on, and vice versa.

Eventually, the officer in charge, who was looking directly into the car, had taken charge of the situation and saved the day.

I learned a lot from that first successful operation that I never forgot in later years. I learned never to rely on those around me to bail me out and I realised I would have to learn to crush any lingering police officer tendencies. Although on this occasion the fact I had pushed Derek to the ground made no difference, in another situation, it could have cost me my life.

The haul of 11 oz. of cocaine was seen as a major coup for the Northern Regional Crime Squad. Derek pleaded guilty and was given four years. Ritchie was picked up on a warrant after the arrests. There was a lot of publicity, with the newspapers and television taking an interest, which kept the buzz of the operation going for a while.

However, the strain of living a double life took its toll on Marianne and she never fully recovered. The fact that we had been left so far out on a limb as a result of a breakdown of communication demonstrated to her how completely alone we were. At the same time, she was in the middle of breaking up with her long-term partner and her mother was dying of cancer. She thought Ritchie was basically a nice guy and felt we had, as a result of our underhand approach, conned him into committing the crime. All these unresolved issues, combined with a lack of any serious counselling, led to her having a nervous breakdown and eventually retiring from the police service on ill-health grounds.

The danger of undercover work had become a reality for me too, but where Marianne found it overwhelming, I was intoxicated by it. My problem was not the thought of going out on another operation, but the tedium of returning to the by now humdrum duties of the Scottish Crime Squad. Having tasted real adventure, more mundane duties such as motorbike surveillance, which had seemed so exciting not so long before, irritated me beyond belief.

Also, not being able to tell your colleagues what you have been doing for the past month is a very isolating experience. Because I had always got on well with them, they would persistently ask what I had been up to, even though they knew I was not supposed to talk about it. And because I was not the kind of person to tell them to mind their own business, I would make something up. If I had been in Newcastle on a drugs bust, I would say I had been in Leeds, buying and selling antiques.

If the success of my first job left me feeling full of myself, however, my second rapidly cut me back down to size. The scenario was basically the same – buying drugs from a dealer – but this time it was not cocaine, but heroin, and the operation was in Manchester, where the gangster scene is heavier and the stakes higher. Using the same legend, I was again to hire a Mercedes, a car I was by now feeling perfectly at ease with, and pass myself off as a fairly major player back in Scotland.

I was told I would be introduced to an Asian man who was 6 ft 4 in. tall with long black hair tied back in a pony tail. Although he was certainly not someone to mess with, he was not amongst Manchester's criminal elite. The idea was that he would introduce me to the people at the top and that the police would subsequently move in and arrest them.

Our first meeting was in a wine bar just outside Manchester. The man was built like Sylvester Stallone and was wearing designer clothes, complete with tight denim jeans and cowboy boots. When I shook hands with him it was as if I was a small boy shaking hands with a grown up. The giant introduced himself as Tony. This guy had a presence about him; he was a confident person. He took control of the meeting, asking all the questions and I felt slightly intimidated. If I had not known better I would have thought he was an instructor from Special Operations 10 (or SO10, Scotland Yard's National Undercover Team) checking my cover story. At one point I had to get a break from him and go to the loo, where I tightened the belt on my trousers and took a long deep breath, reassuring myself I could take control of the situation.

I returned to the table with a different approach. This guy was beginning to piss me off. After listening to Tony's questions and him giving me the instructions as to how we would run the job, I burst and retorted, 'Tony if I did not know any better I could swear you were a cop. For the last hour you have interrogated me about my past, present and future; you are even telling me what way the deal is going to be done. I have not travelled all the way down here to hear this piss. How about shutting the fuck up and let me do some talking.' Much to my surprise the big guy backed down, apologising. After another few hours I realised this guy was a bullshitter; he was well out of his league. I formed the opinion that he was a runner, a gofer, a nobody in the drug scene. This guy was trying to live out his dream as a big player. It turned out that by the end of the evening I had identified him as a bottle merchant under all the height, weight and muscle.

Later that night I returned to my handler and informed him I thought Tony was not in our league and that I didn't think he would be capable of leading us into the bigger players. My handler conveyed my thoughts on to the Manchester Crime Squad. They disagreed and said he was in with the right crowd. My judgement was being called into question. This was a situation I had not been prepared for, a breakdown in confidence between the undercover and the operational teams. They may have been thinking I was not capable and, in turn, I thought their target was not capable. It was a Mexican stand off.

While travelling back to Scotland the following day I told my handler that I thought Tony would make up an excuse not to deal with me as he knew I had seen through his make-up.

I returned to Scotland leaving Tony with my contact number. The ball was in his court. Two weeks later I was told by my handler that Tony had bottled out of the deal. Tony's excuse was that the 'wee Scot' was too heavy for him to handle. The truth was that he knew I had identified him as the muppet in the pecking order of his team.

I learned a valuable lesson from this operation: go with your gut instincts, don't be persuaded by the thoughts of other colleagues, in this case the Crime Squad. It would have been my neck on the chopping block if the job had turned to rat shit, all because Tony had impressed on someone on the squad that he was a big cheese in his team. I do admit, though, that my pride was slightly hurt because I could not pull the job together in Manchester.

Some weeks later another job was to come my way, again in Manchester. While travelling down to the job I felt a little apprehensive at facing the crime squad. However, my fears were to be put to bed when

I was informed by the DI that Tony had been shot by one of his team. Apparently word had got back to the gang boss that Tony, who was a courier for the team, had been trying to branch out on his own. The boss had found out that Tony was skimming some drugs from his deliveries. He would remove a few ounces from the consignment for himself and sell on to another client, probably to me if I had continued dealing with him. This made Tony's boss look as if he was short-changing his clients. Tony was given a warning shot and he was not seriously injured. My gut instinct had been correct.

The Crime Squad wanted me to assist another undercover who had infiltrated a small team of heroin dealers that were working out of a pub in the city centre of Manchester. The undercover was already in and buying deals on a regular basis. My job was to come in as the Scottish dealer looking to source a new supplier for Scotland. My job would be easy as the other undercover had done all the hard work. I had decided I would go in as the man with the money. Again I hired a Mercedes and dressed appropriately.

I met up with the undercover called Trevor. He was a lot younger than I had anticipated. He was in his early 20s and looked it. We spent a night together getting our stories sorted before I was introduced to the dealers.

The following day we met with two of the dealers. I could have been their dad – they were just kids. Again I had that gut feeling that these kids were too far down the pecking order for me to start arranging buys of multi-kilos of heroin. These guys were just starting their apprenticeship in the drugs world.

At the meeting I explained that I was looking for a bigger parcel to 'take up the road' – this being an underworld expression for a large drug deal. These lads asked me to explain. 'I want a couple of kilos to take with me to Glasgow.' The expression on their faces said it all. They were not in such a position to supply my request. After another few ice creams and fizzy drinks with the kids I finally got them to arrange a meeting with their supplier. It was all a bit embarrassing, again I was having to go back and tell my handler I did not think these guys could assist at this present time. I told him that I felt we would need to spend some time moving up the chain of command before getting a larger parcel. Fortunately Trevor agreed with me. It transpired that he had on numerous occasions sounded off to the operational head that these guys were a couple of balloons, so I didn't feel so bad. But, again I returned to Scotland feeling slightly dejected.

Two days later I was sitting in a motorway services awaiting the arrival of a possible target suspected of hijacking articulated lorries. It was my intention to reference myself in and eventually buy one of the hijacked lorries from him. I had contacted him by phone, cold calling, and I was interested to see if he would show.

Eventually this 6 ft 3 in. bruiser appeared and approached me. He introduced himself as John. This guy scared me. He had evil-looking eyes that never blinked. His hair was jet black and over his shoulders. My gut was telling me something but I was too scared to listen.

Forty minutes into the meeting, which was going well, John told me he had just been released from prison. Not wanting to probe too much I asked how long he had been in. 'Life' was the answer. I knew that meant he must have been in for at least 20 years. My gut was talking to me again. I moved on and began trying to pull together a job. John always used the third party when he spoke. He said they could get me a container full of whisky, clothes, food – it all depended on what was there at the time. He told me the container was from England and that the plates would be changed. We talked about money and delivery and finally he asked what I would do with the contents. I told him he didn't need to know. It was at this juncture John said to me, 'That was a copper's reply.'

I froze and he saw the change in my bearing. 'What do you know about coppers?' I asked him.

'I tried to kill one. That's what I got the 25 years for.'

I could feel my blood run cold. I suddenly remembered who this animal was. I could recall the case quite clearly. This guy was a madman.

I lost my train of thought and the will to pull this one together. I just wanted to get up and leave; my bottle was going. I felt I was going off the boil with him and he knew it. I looked at my watch and said we should meet up again to discuss the delivery. Then I left. While driving back to meet my handler my mind was racing. John had the look of a madman in his eyes, he was switched on and had smelt a cop. He didn't give much away but I knew he knew I was a cop. I was not going forward with this one. Again my confidence was knocked.

I was determined I was going to do a job that would put me on the map.

10

OPERATION CLAYMORE

THE TOWN OF Blyth in the North East of England is a desperate place at the best of times. Once a thriving community, the life had drained out of it when the colliery closed, leaving its young men with nothing to do with their time and their energies. While other failing towns were rescued from the brink by the silicon chip, no Japanese companies arrived to bail out Blyth, which, despite the power station that blights its landscape, still has one of the highest unemployment rates in the country. The overcrowded caravan site that perches optimistically on the outskirts of the town and the neat rows of terraced houses, straight from a Lowry painting, all mask the scale of deprivation.

It's the proliferation of junk shops and the back alleys peppered with used needles that tell the true story. Blyth's lack of amenities and prevailing sense of hopelessness make it a perfect breeding ground for a drug problem and by the mid-'90s heroin, methadone, Ecstasy and temazepam, often mixed together in deadly cocktails, were claiming a steady stream of the town's young lives. The dealers plied a successful trade in its many run-down pubs and clubs and its shabby back-street gyms.

However, it wasn't until 1994 and the death of Jenny Hindhaugh – a vivacious, intelligent 16 year old – that the outside world began to take any notice of the town's problems. Jenny's mother, Janette Murphy, was determined that no one else should suffer the same tragedy and launched an anti-drugs crusade. She released a heartbreaking photograph of Jenny wired to a life-support machine that was beamed around the world. In the months that followed a succession of dawn raids were carried out but with little lasting effect. Police officers from the drug squad in Morpeth were banging their heads in frustration. They knew who the major players were but found themselves powerless to touch them. One of those at the sharp end was a Detective Inspector Ben Sanderson, a shrewd old-school police officer who knew just how far to bend the rules in order to get a result. At first sight Ben, who was more than 6 ft, came across as a happy-go-lucky detective but he was one of the sharpest operators I've ever met in my police service; he was suspicious of everybody and always one step ahead of his colleagues. Ben had coordinated the house raids after Jenny's death, when his officers had used their battering rams on as many doors as possible. They had cultivated promising informants but their strong-arm tactics were only successful in the short term. By this time Ben had hatched his plan for undercovers to come and infiltrate the community.

I was looking for a long-term operation to raise my adrenaline levels yet again and I wanted to test my skills. After reflecting on my future during a fortnight's holiday I approached my own handler, John, and explained my feelings to him. John was not an undercover, although he had been on the course as an observer to gain an insight into how the murky world operated. He was, however, a very experienced police officer and commanded my utmost respect. John's job was to coordinate operations I was involved in. He was to take charge of the hiring of cars and other administrative work and he was in control of the purse strings. It was John who told me how much I could spend on a particular job and when I was working south of the border he would liaise with his English counterparts to ensure I kept within the law. It was John who first suggested I might be suited to the Northumberland job, which, unbeknown to us all, would change my whole life.

Ben – who is half Scottish – had decided the officers involved should come from outside the region. He considered the possibility of Londoners then decided it was unlikely a drug dealer from the capital would come up to Blyth for fresh supplies so he opted for Scottish officers. Initially, the sting was to centre on a younger undercover called Gary. Gary would pose as a minor player in the Scottish drug scene who had moved down to Blyth following some fairly heavy domestic bust-ups. Ben and John had looked at Gary's CV and decided he would blend into the community well; this was a lapse in judgement and was to have serious repercussions for both Gary and the operation as a whole. I was to be brought in as Gary's older mate who came to sleep on the floor of his flat from time to time. The operation was to be codenamed 'Claymore', after the large Scottish sword. The success of the operation would depend on support from Ben and a small team of four hand-picked officers. No one else in the force was to be told about our activities, therefore preserving the integrity of the operation but also drastically increasing our chances of being arrested in Blyth.

In August 1996, after John and Ben had met for several secret meetings in the Holiday Inn on the outskirts of Newcastle, Gary was sent on a reconnaissance mission to look for a flat while Ben was tasked with finding him a temporary job to give him a reason to be in the area. Gary picked a luxury flat with an intercom on Croft Road in the middle of Blyth, which was within walking distance of a collection of seedy pubs and surrounded by dead ends and darkened alleys where all sorts of dubious transactions took place. Gary told the landlord he was working as a foreman at the docks and his company was paying for his accommodation. The idea was that when he arrived in Blyth he would say he had been made redundant but that the company had allowed him to stay on in the flat until the end of the year. Next a deal was struck with the managing director of a nearby factory where Gary was to take up a job as a labourer for a few weeks. It was agreed the job would be advertised in the usual way at the local Jobcentre and interviews conducted with other candidates who would be turned down in favour of Gary. Only the managing director was to know the truth about the new worker so that it would be possible for Gary to blend in from the word go.

The first time I met Gary was when we travelled down to the North East to meet Ben and two of his officers for the first time. Throughout the journey we were on a high as we chatted about the job we were about to undertake. This would make our careers, we agreed, it would put us on the map as undercovers and our services would be in demand throughout the country.

In the Holiday Inn we met Neil and Peter, who were to turn out to be two of the closest friends I've had in an outside operation. Neil was in his early 40s, was very quiet, spoke with a broad Geordie accent and sported a thick moustache; Peter was slightly older, wore glasses and had quite an excitable personality. The contrasting personalities of the two men only strengthened their ability as a professional team. They were methodical in their approach to the operation and on occasion went well beyond the call of duty to support us. At this initial meeting a detailed battle-plan was drawn up.

Gary was to live in the flat in Croft Road but would have access to a safe house 30 miles away, near a village called Long Framlington – an idyllic setting a long way from anywhere and yet near enough to the coast. The cottage was to be used to store Gary's personal possessions and for lengthy briefing sessions. Most importantly, it was to serve as a refuge from the stress of his job. It was the only place he could chill out and be himself rather than the criminal who stalked the streets of Blyth.

As Operation Claymore was to be a long-term infiltration rather than a quick hit we didn't want to go in as heavies. Instead we decided to portray ourselves as relatively inexperienced and then once we had been accepted as part of the community we would raise the stakes and strike better and bigger deals. As a result it was decided that Gary should spend most of his time travelling around on a bicycle rather than in a car. Ben said, 'That's what most of the young men are using', and, anyway, it would give him more of an opportunity to strike up conversations with those around him. Also unusually, we were not to be given any particular targets, instead we were told to settle in, talk to as many people as possible, then make our own judgement on who to go for. Once our basic strategy had been established Gary and I spent a few days in the North East just getting to know the place, attuning ourselves to the accent and setting up the flat so it would be ready for him to move in.

The sun was shining as we approached Blyth and my first impression as I went by the caravan park was that the town was a passable seaside resort.

By the time we had turned into the main street, however, the deprivation had become apparent and it began to look more like Easterhouse. It was market day and the town was bustling with harassed-looking mothers jostling to get their hands on the bargains. Almost all the shoppers wore shoes with worn-out heels and had cigarettes hanging out of their mouths. As we drove around the streets surrounding the flat we could see there were junkies lurking in every shadow. The realisation sent a surge of adrenaline through me: there was so much to be done here that we couldn't fail to get a result. Still, I was concerned Gary didn't appear to be responding in the same way.

Gary was the principal character in this drama and yet he was wandering around as if in a trance. I couldn't wait to get in there and was already identifying the pubs that were likely to be our starting point but Gary seemed unable to concentrate and I was concerned he might be getting cold feet. At 24 he was considerably younger than me; he was also better educated and looked like a student with long hair and the friendship bracelet round his wrist. Gary would have the perfect undercover to buy Ecstasy in a nightclub or to put on a trench coat and corduroy trousers and pose as an antiques dealer, but to live six months as a low-level criminal . . . I wasn't so sure. He could swear with the rest of us but from his mouth the words sounded different. It was no reflection on him but in the police service it's horses for courses and I had been worrying for some time that Ben and John had backed the wrong horse. My fear was that under pressure Gary's nerves would collapse and I voiced my reservations to Wendy.

However, the job was Gary's shout. He had been chosen and I wouldn't have considered interfering with that decision. Anyway, I forgot my fears as we approached the flat and I realised that it was almost directly above a second-hand furniture shop, the kind of second-hand shop frequented by thieves off-loading stolen goods. I could almost hear my heart beat with excitement. 'This is where we'll buy the furniture for the flat,' I said but I got no reaction at all; it was clear Gary was on a completely different wavelength. The flat itself was one of eight in a property that was once a cooperative building; it had been bought by a private landlord who had carried out the conversions. Two of the flats, including ours, had controlled entry. Inside, even the hallway was utterly luxurious; it was completely out of place in this run-down part of Blyth. To reach our flat we had to walk along a corridor lined with plaster-cast ornaments. The door opened to reveal an immaculate apartment with pink and peach carpets that looked as though they had never been walked on. There were two double bedrooms and an enormous living room with a kitchenette attached. From the large bay windows at the front of the building you could look out on row upon row of grimy terraced houses and realise you had found an oasis in the desert.

Our first priority was to decide where the technicians should put the covert cameras and other vital equipment, as well as where we should stash the paperwork and the drugs from the deals until we got them back to our handlers. My idea was to hide the camera in the cooker hood so it would shine directly on to a three-piece suite which we would place in the middle of the living room. The suite would also be wired so conversations could be recorded, thus when targets arrived to discuss deals we would be sure of concrete evidence.

After leaving the flat we went straight downstairs to the second-hand shop to introduce ourselves. The owner was a huge man with a crew cut, a tattoo of a spider across his throat, an earring and a face that looked as though it had been hit with a 14-pound hammer. We entered the shop and he gave us a scathing look but when he spoke his manner was friendly enough. He introduced himself to us as Paul. Although Gary was supposed to be the tenant, he hung back as I explained to the shop owner that we were looking for cheap furniture. I then proceeded to give him our cover story, which he seemed to swallow. After having a look around the second-hand furniture store Gary and I made our way to Long Framlington to have a look round the safe house. Gary had picked an immaculate Old English farmhouse with beautiful gardens in which was located the cottage he had rented. The cottage had its own garden and its own private entry. The location was ideal to chill out away from the drugs scene. The intentions were that the inquiry team were going to leave a car at this location for Gary and it would be an unregistered vehicle which Gary could use for his own personal use when he was not working undercover. After exploring

Long Framlington and the surrounding area Gary and I returned to the Holiday Inn where we had a prearranged meeting with Ben. Ben told us that he intended kicking off the job in a fortnight's time and he thought it would be a good idea if Gary and I could have the flat fully furnished and kitted out prior to going live. We agreed.

About a week later, Gary and I returned to Newcastle where we were introduced to Ian – another undercover officer who worked in the Newcastle area. He was a nice guy and fairly experienced in undercover work. He had been told by Ben to assist us in organising second-hand furniture for the flat. We hired a van and Ian told us he had been begging, stealing and borrowing household furniture for our use. The three of us then drove to Northumberland Police Headquarters in Ponteland, where Ian had been storing the goods he had collected. Ian was roughly the same age as me and had a great sense of humour; he was as enthusiastic as me about the job. Unfortunately, we couldn't share this enthusiasm with Gary, possibly because the pressure was now on him and he had to pull the operation together.

At Ponteland headquarters we went to a garage. Ian opened it and found it contained an old three-piece suite that had seen better days. Ian informed us that the suite had been in his grandmother's garage for many years and that it would do us a turn. As we were loading the furniture into the van Gary and I noticed that the suite was covered in blue mould, dog hairs and bird droppings. Ian had been right: the suite would do us a turn – the next turn would be into the second-hand store in Blyth to try and sell it off.

Once the van was loaded we drove back to Blyth and towards the flat. We were unloading the van when Paul came from the second-hand shop and watched us unload our state-of-the-art furniture. As we were removing the settee from the rear of the van Paul stepped forward and said, in his broad Geordie accent, 'I wouldn't let ma fuckin' dog sleep on that,' and laughed. The guy was right, though, and at this juncture I offered to sell it to him. Paul, being the artful dodger, said there was no way he would take it off our hands. I attempted to reciprocate, saying, 'We'll trade it in against a good one that you've got for sale.' This agreed we went and picked a green two-seater settee and two matching chairs. Paul wanted £150 but after some haggling he reduced the price to £130. Gary and I thought we had a good deal until some weeks later I was back in the shop and I noticed the old suite we had just traded lying in the corner with a £95 price tag on it.

With the help of Ian we got the flat looking quite reasonable and it was comfortable to sleep in. We were ready to go. Gary was taking a week's holiday with the view of coming back refreshed. Operation Claymore was about to go live.

11

JUMPING INTO THE BREACH

OPERATION CLAYMORE WAS scheduled to begin on the second Sunday in September. Gary was to spend a week just bumming about his flat before going for the job interview at the factory. I phoned him on Saturday night to wish him good luck and he seemed confident, if a little subdued, as he talked about the task that lay ahead. Just 24 hours later, Gary was lying in a pool of blood in his immaculate bachelor pad having been brutally beaten by a gang in a local pub.

I first heard the operation had run into trouble when John phoned me at home the following day. My immediate feeling was that Gary had been sussed as a police officer by criminals who lost no time in taking their revenge. In fact, since Gary doesn't remember much of the incident, I don't think we'll ever know exactly what happened but his identity did not seem to have been uncovered. It appeared he had gone to a pub and started drinking with some heavies and either he tried unsuccessfully to keep up with his new acquaintances or his beer was spiked with drugs. Certainly he was paralytic by the time the atmosphere turned nasty. A fight broke out either in the pub or just outside it and Gary was kicked repeatedly in the head and stomach and left for dead. Although he was suffering from concussion he managed to stagger back to his flat and throw up everywhere; he then phoned his handler to tell him he was in trouble before collapsing.

The first thing Gary remembered was waking to find his handler standing over him in the hallway; Gary was quivering with fear and was immediately taken to hospital. His leather jacket, bought because it could have concealed a covert camera and some technical equipment was also missing. Ian was giving the plum job of cleaning up the flat.

We all felt demoralised and not a little angry. A lot of time and money had been spent setting up the operation and it had been jeopardised within a day. There was no question of trying to investigate the assault because Gary couldn't remember what pub he had been in or who he had been drinking with. In order to report the matter officially he would have to reveal his identity, a move that would have meant exposing the undercover set-up. At this stage we were completely unsure if Operation Claymore could continue. There was no question of Gary remaining at the flat – his bottle had gone completely and anyway we didn't know to what extent he had been compromised.

On the Tuesday the picture became clearer when Ben phoned me and asked if I would like to step into the breach. Although in retrospect it might seem like the obvious step to take, at the time the suggestion completely took me by surprise. I had assumed that, because Gary was only 24, the operation was perceived as a young man's job but Ben assured me that this was not the case. As I had been involved in setting up the operation, a part of me was thrilled at the prospect of taking on the leading role but there were lots of details to be thrashed out. I wanted to know what financial rewards I would reap for putting my life on the line and more than anything else I wanted to discuss it with my wife Wendy, who, following some discussion, gave me the thumbs up. Obviously I was fazed by what had happened to Gary but there were other factors, such as job satisfaction, to be taken into account.

The financial package, however, was not enticing. I was told that although I would receive an allowance to cover the cost of living and entertaining I would be given only four hours' overtime a day on top of my basic salary. For an operation that was fraught with danger and required round-the-clock commitment this seemed a paltry offering. However, I was impressed by Ben's loyalty and Wendy and I believed an operation of this scale would win me accolades from on high and lead to rapid promotion through the ranks. I accepted the job – not knowing that it would cost me my police career and ultimately my health. It was agreed I would take over where Gary left off, even stepping into his job at the factory, and a week later I was packing a bag with all the clothes I planned to wear during my time there.

Gary had never really given thought to his wardrobe but I remembered from the time that I spent with informants that they all had the same dirty look about them. They wore the same denims, the same shirt and the same trainers day in, day out and they had a kind of musty smell about them. Usually they had three days' growth on their chins and long dirty hair. I wanted to be one of the crowd, to look as dishevelled as them. I spent days at home wearing the same clothes like a method actor trying to get into his role. It could be depressing not taking care of myself, so I decided one day a week I would have a night out where I had washed and changed and felt good about myself. I packed up two suitcases, the first full of Marks & Spencer's jumpers, dress trousers, leather shoes and jewellery – this was for the real me in the cottage in Long Framlington. The second bag was packed full of dirty old gear for my alter-ego in Blyth.

As I stood in my bedroom ready to load the bags into the car I looked in the mirror and saw the reflection of the conflicting aspects of my personality, which had coexisted all these years. The low-level criminal raised in the Gorbals I could so easily have become was about to be recreated in an attempt to tackle the problems caused by the kind of deprivation I had managed to escape all those years ago.

I said goodbye to Wendy and made my way back to the Holiday Inn outside Newcastle, where Ben, Peter and Neil, still shattered by the initial setback, were waiting to brief me, hopeful that I could rescue the operation from its false start. As the linchpin of the operation they gave me a free hand in deciding how to play it out. Of course, Ben had worked in the North East for years and already knew who the key players were but they didn't want to lead me in anyway. I was to work my way into the scene gradually and then start picking off the dealers one by one. If I didn't make any headway after six weeks then they would start directing me. In what felt like a bizarre inauguration ritual I was handed the keys to the flat, the cottage and to the 'death-trap' – a car which Gary had purchased for a paltry £800 and was a traffic officer's dream for every construction and use charge in the book. As I pulled slowly out of the hotel it was like being pushed out to sea on a raft while everyone else watched from the shore.

It was a crisp autumn morning, the sky was a clear blue and my mind was completely focused as I drove the ten miles north to Blyth. I was upbeat about the next six months, although as I passed the caravan site I had to laugh: who in God's name would come on holiday to a cesspit like this? What kind of person was I to give up my home, my family and the scenery of Scotland to bail some chief constable out of a hole? By the time I arrived at the flat, where just days before Gary had lain bruised and bleeding, I had worked myself into a bit of a frenzy. My nerves were frayed, my stomach was churning and I felt worse than I had on any other undercover job I had done before. It was a strange experience. If Ben had arrived on the doorstep and asked me if I wanted to get out I might have said yes, yet at the same time I wanted to be successful and prove worthy of the team's trust.

I was rapidly brought back down to earth, however, by the sight of Paul from the downstairs shop. He was moving furniture in and out of the premises and generally making himself visible to any thieves with stolen goods to offload. This was the first test of my mettle. I had made up a cover story to explain Gary's sudden absence and I had to see if I could tell it convincingly, so I relayed the complicated tale to Paul. Gary's company had moved him from Blyth Docks at short notice to take up a six-month contract in Hong Kong; the company had already paid for the flat and Gary had said I could use it until his return. I told Paul I was a heavy-goods driver in Scotland and that I worked for a family business. I told him the company had gone bust and that I had solicitors up north fighting for a redundancy package for me. I acted a bit lost, not knowing what I was going to do. I was fed up driving and I thought I would stay in Blyth for a while. If I needed some extra cash I would take on a labouring job.

Big Paul was completely taken in by my life story but then why shouldn't he be? He had no reason to suspect I was a police officer. I spoke like a criminal and I had spent some money in his shop – the paltry sum I had spent would blind him to any doubts that he might have had about my story.

Returning to the flat I unpacked the few clothes I had brought with me and then went for my first walk around Blyth, trying to memorise the landmarks and breathe in the atmosphere. The weather was still lovely and everybody in the streets seemed to have a smile on their face. Immediately opposite the flat was a corner shop run by an Asian family that had hardly any stock and looked as if it wouldn't be around for much longer. More promising was my local, the Waterloo Bar. Under extensive renovation, it looked like thousands of other modern pubs, but its clientele appeared to be a little more upmarket than that of other nearby hostelries and I decided that it would be my first and last watering hole of any evening out. I walked in and introduced myself to the manageress, a striking woman whose clothes were just a little too skimpy and make-up just a little too heavy for someone of her age. We had a brief chat, just long enough for her to notice me, and then I made my way back to the flat.

I headed off for a debriefing session with Ben. By this time I was exuding confidence and beginning to feel as if nothing could go wrong. Ben strengthened this sense of my own worth, telling me he was sure I could pull off the operation, but he still had serious matters to discuss. In particular he wanted to make sure I was covered in the event of something going wrong. If I was in danger he said I should just get out of the flat as quickly as possible, ring him from a phone box and he would attend immediately. If the flat was raided by the drugs squad I had to go along with the procedures and allow myself to be arrested and taken down to the police station. Ben warned me about one particular officer whose dedication to the job had won him a large network of informants and as a result faced a realistic prospect of being caught within a CID operation. Such was the officer's notoriety that Ben's warnings were replicated by my criminal acquaintances who warned me not to trust strangers in case they turned out to be his snouts. If the worst should happen, Ben gave me the phone number of a solicitor I could contact; the solicitor was told nothing about my identity but he knew that in the event of my arrest he was to phone Ben immediately.

Back in the flat the technical team had arrived to install the covert cameras and microphones and create safe hiding places. The video was concealed within one of the kitchen units while the covert camera was placed in the cooker hood, as I had anticipated. The system was set: when the intercom buzzed I could look into the street and see who was there, then I could press the switch to activate the tape recorder before speaking the target's name and address to the camera as I let whoever it was over the threshold. One of the kitchen units also contained a false bottom where I could stash the notebooks in which I recorded my every move, my tapes and any drugs I had scored until I could get them safely back to my handlers. It all sounded very professional but it was a while before I was to put the system to the test. First I had to get myself known around Blyth and the best way to do that was to head for the pubs and clubs. I was, however, determined to make a less dramatic entry on the scene than Gary had. I would keep my head down for the first few days at least.

I remember stepping out of the flat into the dark, damp night and feeling a sense of deep isolation descending upon me. The streetlights cast only a faint glow over the back alleys and dead ends that characterised my new home and sinister figures seemed to move in and out of the shadows. I thought of my wife and friends more than two hundred miles away and the English officers in charge of the operation tucked up in the comfort of their own homes and I was momentarily confused by self-doubt. Then I realised I had been limping along with one foot on the pavement and one in the gutter so I could run into the middle of the road if someone jumped out of a doorway with a knife. I shook myself out of my lurid imaginings. There was no reason for anyone to suspect I was a police officer and as long as I didn't come on too heavy I would be safe. I decided I would only speak to my fellow drinkers if they spoke to me first, so as not to appear too conspicuous. If a barmaid appeared friendly I would strike up a conversation about places to go and those to avoid but I wouldn't advertise my presence. Feeling slightly more confident I made my way to my local, the Waterloo Bar, where I had a pint of bitter and a whisky chaser to steady my nerves. It was quickly clear, however, that the Waterloo, although an oasis of light and warmth for me, was an unlikely haunt for drug dealers. I quickly moved on through a relentless stream of spit and sawdust joints, eyeing up all the drinkers and trying to judge the most likely targets.

On the way home I contacted Wendy. She was apprehensive, wondering what her man was walking into; I'd taken a fair bit to drink and my voice betrayed my worries. When I look back on the operation now I see it was a terrible thing to have put my family through. After reassuring Wendy that everything was fine and I was comfortable and safe, I walked back to the flat. It was a strange feeling walking into an empty flat with bare bulbs. I made myself some tea and toast and tried to relax. I could actually feel my body tense, I could hear shouting and car doors slamming somewhere outside; it was a barrage on my senses. When I had been involved in other undercover jobs I had always stayed in plush hotels and driven a fancy car, I'd never stayed near the targets and I had certainly never lived on the job. I was now cocooned on the job that was going to be part of my life for the next six months. That night I didn't sleep well, I was up and down and tossed and turned. The first night was a night I would like to try and forget.

I was drifting off to sleep when the phone rang at 7.30 a.m., as it would at that time every morning from then on. Ben, who was always in the office early, would call to see if I had made it through the night. Throughout the time that I spent in Blyth the sound of his voice was to prove reassuring, a touchstone in my increasingly chaotic existence. After pulling on the same dirty jeans I had worn the day before, I got myself out on the street like a good community police officer. I would tread the beat until I knew every inch of the streets around my flat and the face of every person who lived around there.

It was a good time of the morning to be out and about. The junkies — coming down from last night's high — were emerging, ashen-faced, in search of their next score. Those who lived from day to day on a methadone substitute were loitering outside chemists, waiting for the shutters to go up, while others were making their way to the dole office to sign on. Later on in the day I would spend some time in the bookies where a handful of junkies and thieves hung out. I would then float from pub to pub to single out any illegal activities going on.

By lunchtime most of the pubs would be filled with shoplifters and thieves shifting their gear. A hi-fi out of a car or a CD from Woolworth's would be bought and sold under the table. Any intelligence I gathered, no matter how seemingly insignificant, I passed on to Ben, either to act on that day or to store away for future reference. All the time my face was getting known. I spent a lot of time in the second-hand shop below the flat talking to Paul and his young gofer, Brian, who was a likeable chap. Brian was nothing like Paul. He was not involved with the underworld so could not introduce me to any great contacts but he was a football fan and I used our encounters to learn about Newcastle United. The knowledge I gained from Brian was essential in a part of the country where an awareness of the club is one way of guaranteeing yourself in on any conversation. Paul was to prove more useful but also more tricky because he never stopped asking questions. Later I was to find out he had some friends within the police force.

At the end of the first week I had a meeting with Ben in the safe house, where much to my relief I was allowed to spend the weekend with Wendy. There I could wear my own clothes and travel about as I wished but I still couldn't entirely relax as I had been forced to adopt yet another identity. The farmer who owned the cottage had naturally been curious about the short-term lease so we told him I was a sales rep covering a hundred miles north and south of Newcastle and I needed a central base for occasional meetings with clients and colleagues. Even on my day off I had to assume another identity. I had now developed three personalities: my original life as David Corbett, which was retained in the farmhouse in Long Framlington; the cover story of being the sales rep; and the criminal in Blyth.

At the meeting I told Ben that I thought the bedding-in period had gone well, with people already beginning to nod at me in the street. The only thing that worried me slightly was that someone had sprayed the word 'wanker' over the car Gary had left for me and the tyres had also been slashed. It might have been a coincidence but it made me uneasy to think Gary had made enemies that might come after me and since I was not allowed to contact Gary there was no way of finding out. In any case, the car was eating up petrol and looked as if it would give up the ghost at any minute.

Ben told me a labouring job had finally been sorted within a nearby upholstery factory. As planned, I was to go to a nearby Jobcentre where the position had been advertised, avoiding the possibility of arousing any suspicions amongst the rest of the factory workforce. So on Monday I went straight there and picked up the card and took it to the desk. When the girl behind the counter asked for my details, I said I was new to the area and I had been a self-employed driver before moving to Blyth. I couldn't use the redundancy story this time because she would have asked for my P45. She raised her eyebrows a little but nevertheless sorted out an interview for the following day.

I was the fifth person on the managing director's list and although I had already been promised the job I would have to sit in line before being summoned into his office. I tried to imagine what a labourer would wear and say. It was all getting very complicated – I was beginning to feel as if I was a schizophrenic with multiple personalities and pasts. The trick was to make sure the right me always appeared at the right moment. The factory was situated in a large industrial unit with offices and a showroom. I had to register with the secretary and wait out in the foyer until my name was called. The minute I passed through the door, however, the temperature thawed slightly. 'Thank God you're here,' the managing director said. 'I'm sick of interviewing people who weren't going to get the job.'

I smiled but I had to be careful not to come across as too friendly, as the office was a goldfish bowl with employees throwing curious glances in our direction to see what was going on. I assured the managing director I was there only to give myself a legitimate reason to be in Blyth and that I would do whatever I was told throughout my weeks there. He told me I would be sweeping the shop floor and would be paid cash at the end of the week for my troubles. We shook hands on the deal and agreed that my brief, glittering career as a factory worker would begin the following week.

12

THE BENGAL TIGER

AT A LOOSE end I decided to spend some more time with Brian. Paul was away for a few days and this was an opportunity to win Brian's trust without any interference from his boss's prying eyes. We seemed to have a rapport going, so later that afternoon I asked him if he knew where I could buy some dope as a friend was coming down for the weekend and we fancied a bit of a smoke. Brian seemed a little taken aback but he said he might be able to sort me out the next time I was in. I was sure he knew who the main players were.

The following day I was standing washing my car, watching the passing trade, when Brian approached me. 'That man at the end of the street is the one who can sell you the cannabis,' he said and at those words my heart just leapt. I was on the verge of setting up my first deal to infiltrate the drugs network – albeit a deal of cannabis. For a fleeting second I felt sorry for Brian, who was a harmless lad. When the operation was over and the arrests made the criminals would sit down and try to analyse who brought me in to the circle and the trail possibly would lead back to him. At the same time he was clearly, knowingly, involved in the supply of drugs and that in itself was a serious offence. I knew I would need Brian's help if I was to win the dealer's trust. I asked him to do the necessary introductions; reluctantly he pulled the shutter down on the shop and I drove him down the road to where the man was standing. As we got closer I saw that the young lad was bow-legged and had scars down the side of his face. Brian rolled the car window down and gestured to him to come over. 'Begsie,' he said, 'I want to introduce you to my friend Dave.'

Begsie leaned menacingly through the window, clearly cagey about getting too deeply involved with someone he didn't know. I could almost hear him thinking, 'What are you doing bringing this wildcard to me?' He insisted he had no gear on him. I asked if I could take him to his house and remarkably he agreed. We went to his home, which was an upstairs flat in a row of terraced houses. The flat was devoid of furniture and carpets, and while I waited for him to make his move a tiny kitten ran around the bare floorboards, meowing softly. Begsie opened the kitchen drawer and brought out a piece of cannabis. I gave him £15 and the deal was done. Suddenly we were all laughing and joking. Begsie was asking me how long I had been in Blyth and I was offering to buy him a pint at the first opportunity. I was euphoric; it was as if I had landed one million pounds of heroin. On my tenth day in Blyth, Operation Claymore had taken off and I had my first real target. It was a rush that I had never experienced on any other operation but then I had never before lived amongst the people I was trying to incriminate before.

I couldn't wait to phone the operations room but frustratingly Ben's number was ringing out. I left an excited message with Neil and hurried back to the flat to stash the drugs in my safe and to start writing the first page of my first notebook. It was a momentous moment, from now on in every target would have his own notebook and I would have more than 30 on the go by the end of the operation. The only downside to my first deal was that it was so early in the operation and the car was giving us so much trouble that neither I, nor the car, was wired and I had no corroborating evidence of the transaction. However this did not worry me unduly as it was already clear that Begsie was to play a central role in my new life and money would be changing hands on a regular basis. Strangely, although throughout the operation I was to see Begsie every second day I didn't know his real name until he stood in court with all the others at the conclusion of the operation when he was charged with dealing.

By arrangement I was to meet Neil at 5 p.m. in the public toilets near to the seaside resort of Seaton Sluice. This meeting point had been chosen because of its reputation as a gay haunt and the sight of two men entering the toilets at the same time would not be out of place. Neil got out and shook my hand to congratulate me. I handed over the cannabis with great ceremony and it was placed in a plastic exhibit bag and logged. Neil told me that Ben had done some digging: Begsie was well known locally as a bit of a hard man and he was also known to the police. I was heading in the right direction. Ben also promised he would sort out the problems with the car over the next week or so.

Returning to Blyth, I felt I deserved a few beers and headed to the Waterloo Bar. I bumped into a man called Nigel – a former soldier, now gas fitter – who lived above me in Croft Road. Nigel turned out to be the barmaid's boyfriend. At first he was a bit standoffish with me, wary because he couldn't understand how I could be unemployed and living in a flat that cost £400 a month. The good news was he had a passion for motorbikes and when he discovered I shared his enthusiasm the barriers immediately came down. Although he was not involved in drugs at this time it soon became clear he had his finger in a lot of pies and could be a useful source of information. Drink had loosened his lips and he was soon telling me how he had broken his leg in a fight in a pub a few weeks earlier and was now off work. I began to wonder if Gary had been involved in the same fight. I wasn't exactly sure what Nigel was dabbling in but I was going to make it my job to find out.

The following day I decided to tell Brian I had a mate coming up from London who was looking to do some cocaine. Brian said he knew someone who lived close by and that he would try and set up an introduction. Later that day Brian came through and gave me an address. I was told to turn up at the address, knock on the door and introduce myself as a Scots guy who was looking for some gear. It was a very strange scenario for me as my previous jobs had always involved big players, but this time I was working at street-level, on people's doorsteps, which was in some ways is even more dangerous.

This time I went home and got myself wired before walking the 50 yards to the dealer's home in Bernard Street. I knocked on the door as instructed and it was answered by an attractive woman in her mid-30s. 'Brian told us you would be calling,' she said, introducing herself as Anne. She was very cautious and my instincts told me to back off. However I kept pushing.

'My friend is desperate to score,' I said, 'can you help us? You can come over to my flat if you want to check me out.'

Anne let me in to her front room where her partner Wayne was sitting in his boxer shorts. The house was moderately decorated, immaculately clean and everyone was very polite. I began to feel more comfortable. In the corner a girl aged about seven or eight was sitting quietly in her school uniform doing her homework. I sat down and Wayne offered me a joint. I declined, explaining I had work to do but would take a smoke later on in the day. Anne went away and came back with the deal for which I paid her £20. Wayne admitted he had been involved in some armed robberies and I said I had done a bit of that in my youth but had put it behind me as I grew older. I was almost at the door, ready to leave, when I asked Wayne what drugs he used.

'We're both registered heroin addicts,' he said matter of factly.

I couldn't believe it. To look at their home and their children you would have thought they were a steady, respectable family, not junkies who spent most of their lives trying to score their next fix. Confirmation of Anne and Wayne's reputation came the following day when Paul approached me and warned me to be careful about the company I was seen in. It was strange Paul saw me as a cut above Wayne and Anne. He said if I was seen walking in and out of the house my card would be well marked with Northumbria Police. Inwardly I smiled but appeared to take his advice seriously. Thanking him for his concern, I told him I had only gone there because my friend was desperate and I would try to keep my distance in the future.

That weekend I went home to see Wendy and my daughters. I was exhausted but bursting to tell Wendy all about the inroads I had made in Blyth and about the labourer's job I would be starting the following week.

The weekend over I returned to Blyth, eager to start my new job. Just as on my first day as a probationer, I arrived at the upholsterer's factory 15 minutes early on Monday morning so I could get a good look around and get the measure of the place. I quickly worked out that the factory workers were set on three levels in a kind of class structure. On the very bottom rung were the pattern cutters whose jobs were simply to take a pair of scissors to the material. Next were the sewers who stitched the material into the appropriate shape and the top were the upholsterers who walked with a John Wayne swagger and saw themselves as the crème de la crème. As a floor-sweeper I was the lowest of the low; my job was to empty bins full of wood and material into a baling machine and to brush up around them. This was all I did day in day out but of course my real task was to keep my ear to the ground and work out who the players were. In addition, the managing director, who had arranged the posting, asked me as a favour to root out any ineptitude or corruption in respect of his workforce for his information only. I was happy to do this but as it became increasingly apparent the managing director was hated, I kept my distance to offset any suggestions of favouritism. Some of the workforce noticed my old car and very quickly started muttering jibes under their breath. Time and time again I explained I was only working as a labourer to tide me over until more heavy-goods-vehicle work came my way but they remained sniffy about my lowly station.

The snobbery amongst the upholsterers manifested itself in my first tea break when a worker at the same table as myself started dealing a hand of cards to everyone bar me. It was hard to take, knowing that I was at the peak of my career and being treated like scum by people who had never stuck their necks out in their lives. After several days of being cut out of the card games I demanded to be dealt in but my request was treated with outrage. The dealer told me politely but firmly that upholsterers and labourers do not mix socially as upholsterers were professional craftsmen. At the back of my head a voice kept telling me not to get involved in a confrontation so early on but I couldn't help myself. I stood my ground. I looked straight at him, unflinchingly, until he became uncomfortable and then I said, 'I'm a lorry driver, not a labourer.'

There was a deathly silence for a second or two and then the upholsterer relented. 'I suppose you're just passing through as a labourer,' he said and from that moment I was accepted.

This meant I was one of the few people in the factory who could float in and out of the camps talking to everyone and because of this I quickly identified that a couple of labourers were working a scam that allowed them to steal material. The scam was simple; they placed what they wanted in a black bag and then, marking the bag, placed it in the skip in such a way that when they returned later that night it could be easily retrieved.

During the first week I was approached by management and asked if I wished to do overtime. Like hell I did – my routine of baling and putting rubbish in skips was hard work for £130 per week. It certainly made me appreciate my job within the police force. I didn't realise how lucky I was. By the time Friday came I was feeling very tired. I was keeping long hours, getting up at 6.30 a.m., travelling to the factory, working until 5.30 p.m., returning to my flat around 7.30 p.m. and preparing myself to go out and socialise in the evening. During this time I was also having regular meetings with the inquiry team. At my next meeting with Ben I told him the job at the factory was taking a lot out of me. I felt that working in the factory and also trying to source targets was too much. Ben agreed and, as I had been unable to identify possible players within the factory, I decided I would hand my notice in at the first opportunity.

I returned to work on the Monday morning and put the word round the guys on the shop floor that I was possibly going to come into redundancy money from my previous job in Scotland. The seed was now planted and nobody would be surprised if I walked off the job. On Wednesday of that week I had reached the end of my tether, putting in long hours and receiving nothing for them other than working in the factory for eight hours a day. I felt now was the time to hand in my notice. It gave me great pleasure at lunchtime to walk into the managing director's office and tell him I was leaving. I told him Ben would contact him and fill him in with the information and intelligence that I had gathered. I felt a massive weight had been removed from my shoulders. I was now going back to do the job that I had really come to Blyth to do.

That afternoon I returned to the flat and received a telephone call from Ben who informed me that he had been given a budget to purchase another vehicle. I contacted Ian, the undercover officer who had helped Gary and I move into the flat. Ian and I met up and went car hunting and within a couple of hours we purchased a silver, four-door, automatic Ford Granada 2.8 Injection Ghia X. It was a dream machine, the previous owner having to sell the vehicle due to financial commitments. The car was obviously the previous owner's pride and joy and was immaculate.

Later that day, having paid £1,000 cash for the car, I drove back into Blyth. I felt like 'the Man' as I drove back into Croft Road and parked outside the flat. Paul came out of his shop. He showed great interest in the vehicle and even more in how much I had paid for it. I told him I was now in the money as my redundancy had come through from Scotland and I intended spending some of the money in his shop, reorganising my flat with some modern furniture. This brought a smile to the fat boy's face.

In the flat I reflected on the day's work; it had been a good day and I was relieved that the job in the factory was now over. I could now start concentrating and putting my energy into pulling the operation back together. In hindsight it was a good idea to have had the reference of the factory but it wasted weeks of the operation. Later that night I decided to call in to see Anne and Wayne, hoping to score again. When I went round to the house, Anne answered the door and informed me that Wayne was out. I asked her if she could help me as I was looking for a piece of tack (cannabis). Anne apologised and said that she was not in a position to help. However, she did offer to take me to a guy she knew by the nickname of Segs. Anne asked me into the house while she got ready to go out.

After a few minutes of small talk I was driving through Blyth to Disraeli Street. It was a dark, cold winter night and the streets were poorly lit; this was not the most salubrious area of Blyth. Anne told me to stop the car outside an end-of-terrace house, which was split into flats; the upstairs flat appeared uninhabited. This, she said, was where Segs and his girlfriend lived. She got out of the car and knocked on the door and her knock was met by the almighty roar of a large dog barking and snarling. A few moments later the door was opened by a female who Anne engaged in conversation, pointing towards my car. A few minutes later Anne came down and told me that Segs was out but his girlfriend now knew my car and was aware I would be calling at a later date to pick up some tack, if and when Segs had gear in the house. Anne apologised that she couldn't get me sorted. I drove her back home and returned to my flat where I created a notebook in the name of Segs.

Later that night I called again at Segs's place. When I knocked on the door I was met by an Alsatian the size of a pit pony with teeth on it like a Bengal Tiger. The girl Anne had spoken to answered the door; she recognised me but said she still did not have any gear. I decided to put my police training back into practice and take observations of the house from a short distance. I watched the house for about ten or fifteen minutes from a discreet location some streets away and I was pleased to see numerous callers being turned away like I had been. I knew then I hadn't been sussed and would be able to return to the door at some later date.

It had been another long day and I decided to lock up the flat for the night and drive out to the safe house for a quiet drink in a local village pub where nobody knew me as an undercover police officer or as a would-be drugs dealer. About 7 p.m. I left the flat and decided I would have one more go at Segs's flat before heading towards the safe house. I was determined I was going to get a score to finish what had been a reasonably good day. I knocked on the door and, as on the previous occasion, the Alsatian came snarling downstairs, attempting to push its muzzle through the letterbox and bite the unsuspecting caller. This time the door opened and a man stood in front of me. I introduced myself as being a friend of Anne and Wayne's and he introduced himself as Segs. He told me that his girlfriend had told him about the intro from Anne and he was comfortable to invite me into his house. Segs had the dog by the collar; I was now entering the proverbial lion's den, or should I say the Bengal Tiger's den.

Segs directed me upstairs and told me to turn first left into the living room. I was slightly uncomfortable with the position I was placing myself in – it was just a deal I was looking for, I didn't want any trouble. Segs told me that he didn't have any tack. He was waiting on the delivery, which he said would be arriving in the next five or ten minutes, and asked me if I was prepared to wait. I was now committed and to keep face I decided to settle down inside the house and wait. I was thinking to myself that at least I'd record good evidence as my technical equipment, which thankfully I was wearing, would pick up the conversation we were having. Segs led me into the sparsely furnished living room – typical of some of the drug dealers in the area. I found his large wide-screen television and matching video ironic, placed amongst the threadbare carpet, the table and chairs in the corner and the suite that had seen better days. I could possibly have advised him where to buy a second-hand suite in the Blyth area if the conversation arose. Segs then went on to explain that his supplier had fucked up with his delivery and the stuff would be with us shortly. I said it was not a problem but I could only wait ten or fifteen minutes as I had a mate arriving from London and I didn't want to be away from the flat too long.

The picture was now painted. I was sitting comfortably with the Alsatian at my feet, snarling and showing its teeth, while Segs was in the kitchen looking out the window, waiting for his courier to arrive. His wife was not the best conversationalist in the world, so I was saying nothing, just looking straight ahead, while Segs was nervous because he had a stranger in his home and his supplier had let him down drastically. I found it hard trying to make conversation. I spoke about the dog, which after ten or fifteen minutes eventually settled and accepted me as part of the surroundings. The dog moved closer and laid its head on my lap with its nose resting on my crotch. Forty-five minutes later I could feel the sweat running down the back of my underpants. Questions began to run through my head: How long does the tape run for? If the tape switches off will it make a buzzing noise? When will it run out? The Alsatian was now concentrating on my lower privates – obviously the dog had sensed that I was getting nervous and on smelling fear, it moved closer to my crotch. Could the dog actually hear the tape going round inside my underpants? A million things ran through my head; panic was now setting in. Should I get up and leave? Should I kick the dog in the balls? Or should I sit it out? I knew that if the tape switched off it could blow the whole operation. Time was getting on and I hadn't expected to be this long.

Segs entered the room. 'No problem, mate, everything's cool. Just sit tight, be comfortable.'

I explained to him that I would need to leave shortly as my mate would be standing outside the flat. He reassured me that the commodity that was about to arrive was the best; he kept saying, 'Just hang fire, sit where you are.'

My mind was like a runaway train: 'Whatever the fuck happens, Dave Corbett, you should remember your training days, always check your equipment.' This was a situation I didn't need, sitting in a house with a tape on, a dog's head in my lap and knowing that I was going to blow the whole operation if my tape switched off. My stomach was now like a washing machine. I was trying to control my Adam's apple from going up and down and the dog's head was buried deeper in my crotch. 'God Almighty, hurry up, deliver the bloody drugs. Please, God, please.'

While this was all going around in my head I had missed the courier entering the kitchen and dropping off two large soap-bar deals of tack. Within a few seconds Segs had cut me my piece. I had given him the money and we exchanged pleasantries. I was out of there, safe. I returned to the car and immediately gave a quick résumé to the tape of what had taken place. I knew the operation team would hear the panic in my voice. The episode brought it home to me that this was not an exercise being run by SO10, this was a live operation and the stakes were getting higher.

13

MY FIRST HIT

PRIOR TO TAKING up duties within Operation Claymore I had been reasonably fit and I had been attending the gym on a regular basis. I had always been fairly active in one sport or another, be it five-a-side football, swimming or jogging. Since coming to Blyth I hadn't visited a gym or been involved in any sort of training. This was due to the long hours and the heavy drinking. I now decided it was time to try and get my body back into shape. With this in mind I made enquiries at a local gym which was approximately 500 yards from where I lived. As I walked towards the gymnasium I wrongfully expected it to have the type of equipment I had been used to back home: state-of-the-art treadmills with electronic cross trainers and walls of television screens which you could watch while taking your mind off the pain and burning off the fat.

When I entered the gym in Blyth I took a walk back into the 1950s. There were no modern machines. The only equipment this gymnasium had were bar bells, benches, sit-up machines and pulleys. I had walked into a body builder's gym as opposed to a gym where you would come and work out and have a relaxing afternoon. The owner, known as Popeye, approached me. He was 5 ft 5 in. in height and measured 6 ft from one shoulder to the other, with a crew-cut hairstyle. We exchanged pleasantries and I yet again relayed my cover story. I told Popeye my intention was to work out and possibly lose some weight. There was a second reason which I would not disclose to him: it was my intention to see if there were any players using the gym. Amphetamine was always a favourite drug of those trying to enhance their body or increase their stamina in sport. Amphetamine or speed enhanced weight loss. It was a shot in the dark, but meant I could kill two birds with one stone: get fit and possibly identify some more targets. My intention was to visit the gym on a regular basis, possibly every day, time permitting.

Ben had an ingenious idea to purchase Pringle jumpers at cost and sell them to selective targets with a view to increasing my credibility. It was also suggested by the operational team that we do the same with whisky. So Ben purchased 60 Pringle jumpers and 20 bottles of whisky. I now had a commodity in which I could deal and play off against other targets.

The following day I returned to Popeye's gym where he talked me through the equipment, not that there was much to learn in respect of lifting weights. Over the next week I built up a rapport with Popeye and by the end of the week he knew everything about me except my national insurance number and that I was an undercover cop. I saw many faces coming and going from the gym, however I didn't see any illicit drug trading or dealing going on.

Popeye was a strange character. He kept two large kestrels in his small office, off the training floor. Only those he trusted were invited into his den. I felt now would be the time to introduce some jumpers and booze to Popeye as he was beginning to feel comfortable in my company. I invented a story that I had come into jumpers that had been stolen from a golf club in Scotland. Popeye took the story on board and asked how much I was selling them for. We agreed on a price and he took a dozen jumpers from me. I didn't accept money at that time but I said I would call back later. After about ten days I decided that enough was enough and I was pulling away from Popeye's gym. It was my intention to see if Popeye would seek me out and I had an ace card up my sleeve if he did.

The operation was going well. I had, as they say in the trade, bagged Segs, I had obtained another few deals from him and Ben had instructed me now to pull away as they had enough evidence to secure a conviction. I had also been visiting Anne and Wayne on a regular basis and I was now collating useful information about them. Wayne had freely admitted that he was a cat burglar and was responsible for breaking into houses in the Blyth area. Anne also admitted that she was involved in 'kiting', which was the local term for using stolen credit cards and committing fraud. They both asked if I would be prepared to drive them into the centre of Newcastle with a view to them committing frauds with me as their chauffeur. I asked Ben his advice on this one and he asked me to back off slightly – we were now getting involved in realms of agent provocateur. Anne and Wayne had a young son called Scott, who, when I first met him, I would have estimated to be about 14 or 15. He was about 4 ft 10 in., very pale and drawn, and, much to my surprise, was actually 19 years of age. I was later to find out that he was a prolific shoplifter. Every snippet of information that Anne and Wayne gave me I fed back to Ben who built a dossier and passed on to the relevant departments within Northumbria Police.

I continued to associate with Paul and Brian in the second-hand shop. During one of my visits I was introduced to another Brian, who I nicknamed BJ (Brian the Junkie). BJ was a young lad in his early 20s, who was obviously educated and had come from a good home before the Devil's powder (heroin) had taken its toll. He was now a £40-a-day habit man. Often when I went into Paul's shop BJ would be standing talking and my guess was that he was moving on stolen property to Paul, although this was never confirmed. I longed for the opportunity to spend some time with BJ on his own because I was more than convinced he would lead me into bigger and better things. BJ was hungry for cash and I could possibly put some his way if he led me in the right direction.

I was very interested in dealing with Paul but he gave me no signals that he was a player until one day, while I was washing my car – my pride and joy, the Granada – Paul approached and drew my attention to the tax disc which had expired two months previously. It was part of my cover that I would flaunt the law now and again. Paul said that I was lucky I hadn't been stopped by the plod. I told Paul that I hadn't received my full redundancy and if and when the money came through it would be the next investment. Much to my surprise, Paul said that he could possibly get his hands on an

MOT certificate and a tax disc. I almost bit his hand off at the offer. Paul said he would come back to me at a later date and, true to his word, some days later he produced a tax disc and MOT certificate. At that time there were no questions asked; the tax disc was duly placed on the windscreen of my car and the MOT certificate was handed over to Ben for further investigation. In return for the favours rendered by Paul I offered him some of the whisky for sale. He gladly accepted the offer and we now had a common trust.

A few days later I was driving through Blyth when I observed BJ walking. I seized the opportunity and stopped and offered him a lift. BJ told me he was going back to his flat as he had some business to do, from which I read that he was going to inject his newly purchased smack. While en route I spun BJ the sad story that I was having friends down from Scotland and that I needed some tack. I mentioned that my supplier in Blyth did not have any and asked if he could suggest anywhere. BJ suggested I call back for him in half an hour and he would introduce me to someone; I gladly accepted his invitation.

Thirty minutes later I returned as promised to BJ's address. When BJ emerged from the front door of his mid-terraced flat he had the tell-tale signs of having just injected heroin: he was slightly unsteady on his feet, his eyes were glazed and his speech was slurred. BJ got into the car and told me to drive. We had driven for about five minutes when we reached our destination, which was a newly built mid-terraced row of houses just outside the centre of Blyth. BJ told me prior to getting out of the car that he would introduce me to the guy. He said the guy was a bit of a nutter and I was to stay cool should anything happen. Again my mind ran riot.

BJ knocked on the door, which was answered by a small, lean, fit-looking man in his mid-50s. BJ slurred his words and told him that he was looking for some gear. The man, seeing BJ was under the influence, immediately blew up, shouting and swearing and pointing at him, calling him a 'fucking junkie head'. On seeing me standing slightly back from BJ he kicked off again, shouting and swearing and saying, 'Who the fuck is that?' and asking why BJ was bringing strangers to his door. The guy then slammed the door shut in BJ's face.

It was at this juncture I decided to make my move, I pulled BJ out of the way and I told him to sit in my car. For some reason I had now moved into overdrive. I knocked on the door and again the door was answered by the tyrant whose veins were now sticking out of his neck. In my quiet Scottish voice I told him to cool down, using my hands as a fan as if I was damping down flames. I could see the veins on the guy's neck slowly disappear, he then apologised and began to explain that BJ was a junkie and that he didn't like him coming around his house. I went on to explain that Brian was only doing me a good turn and again proceeded to tell my tale of woe, my cover story. The guy shook my hand and invited me in. As I entered the hallway and climbed the stairs to an unknown destination I could hear voices within. After seeing this guy's temper I began to think twice about whether I had done the right thing.

I entered the living room where I saw five teenagers sitting. They were all smoking what appeared to be tack (cannabis). The householder was now back on planet earth and again shook my hand and introduced himself as Jay. Jay seemed quite a likeable guy when the veins in his neck were not protruding. He asked me exactly what I wanted and I told him I was looking for a piece of tack. Jay said that he didn't do tack, however he did do grass or weed. I joked and said, 'Beggars can't be choosers. I'll take what you've got.' Jay left the room and returned a short time later with a clear polythene bag, which had approximately 50 or 60 deals of grass individually wrapped and placed inside. Jay told me to take one; obviously I had to ask the price first. The price was £15 and I could take whatever one I wanted.

After doing the deal I decided it was time to return to my car, if it was in fact still there and BJ hadn't gone off with it or sold the wheels. On returning to the car BJ was very apologetic. He genuinely appeared embarrassed at having put me in that position. From my experience, if BJ continued in his drug abuse he would not have long to live. His mouth, which had once contained a row of well-polished molars, was now displaying teeth that would have made Steptoe's father proud. He was a sad-looking individual. The human side of me began to feel sorry for him.

I remember one of the lecturers at SO10 telling us the story of the Stockholm Syndrome. Patty Hurst, a female who had been kidnapped in the

Stockholm area by terrorists, was held captive for a long time and eventually became sympathetic to the cause and in fact a terrorist herself. Was I thinking that way? Was I falling into the trap of the Stockholm Syndrome? I had to pull myself back into check and remember that drugs had turned BJ into a thief and a drug dealer. I soon realised that one of the hardest things in being alone undercover was that your mind sometimes plays tricks on you, you end up looking deeper into events, conversations and indeed your own personality. I had to stop this or eventually it would drive me over the edge. I dropped BJ off and returned to the flat.

Ben called me to say that his intentions were now to introduce another undercover as we had previously discussed. The decision had been made to bring in another Scots guy who would pose as my brother, Vinnie. I had already planted the seeds with some of the dealers by describing my brother as a smack-head or a heroin addict and mentioning that he was coming to stay with me. At this time I wasn't aware who would play the role of Vinnie, however it was good news that he was to be a fellow Scot. Apparently Vinnie had a wealth of experience in dealing with drugs and had been in numerous drug squads. He had just passed his course at SO10 and this was to be his first operation. I felt comfortable knowing that I would be working with a fellow Scot and knowing that, as an experienced officer, he wouldn't let me down.

In the middle of that week I received a call from Ben that I had to attend a meeting at the safe house. Vinnie had arrived. One half of me was excited that I was going to have company and the other part was apprehensive that somebody might cock up and spoil the whole job. When I arrived at the cottage Vinnie was there with his handler, as were Ben, Neil and Peter; the atmosphere was good. Ben's team were now comfortable in my company and we were having a good laugh. Ben had a very dry sense of humour and on some occasions his own team didn't know whether he was taking the piss or being serious. I liked Ben's style and I couldn't have wished for a better operational head.

It was good to see Vinnie, who had even dressed for the role. Vinnie was unshaven and by the looks of things hadn't put a brush through his hair in the last two days. He had the regulation shellsuit and trainers, a T-shirt, sweat-top and a hooded jacket – if I hadn't known he was a police officer I would have considered him a junkie. Vinnie was briefed by Ben and then we were on the road. The drive back to Blyth gave me time to fill Vinnie in on exactly what had been done prior to his arrival on the job. He was nervous when we first drove into Blyth, as I had been, and we toured around so I could show him some of the locations I had visited. I could see in his eyes that he was as excited as I was. Vinnie settled into the flat well, as he had very few belongings with him other than a spare pair of underpants and socks. The intention was that he would stay for two or three days and then move on and return in a couple of weeks. Vinnie knew my legend inside out and he then narrated his; fortunately we were both of similar appearance and stature.

That evening we decided to have a meal in the flat and then take a walk round some of the local hostelries. While I was cooking dinner I asked Vinnie if he would go to the local grocer's and collect a few cans of lager. He appeared apprehensive at first and on leaving the flat I opened the curtains to watch his safe passage to and from the local grocer's. I watched as Vinnie walked up the centre of the road and returned by the same route, and when he entered the flat I asked, 'Why were you walking in the centre lines?'

Vinnie laughed nervously and said, 'The shadows scared me. I'm not comfortable in this place just now.'

I laughed and shared my experiences of my first night on the job with him. I had to reassure him that his confidence would come and that everything was cool. That evening he and I bummed around the local pubs in Blyth and I introduced him to some of the characters I'd already met.

The following morning we decided that I would call at BJ's house and tell him that as my brother had arrived we required some kit so he could score. Vinnie remained in the flat familiarising himself with the technical equipment. I called at BJ's house on Union Street and after several loud attempts at trying to waken the dead from within he answered the door. BJ was still wearing the clothes he had on the previous day and by the look of him he had been sleeping in them.

The terraced house was an upper flat, which consisted of four rooms, all of which had been converted into bed-sits. I entered BJ's bed-sit and looked around. There was no floor covering, the bed was adorned by a duvet which had seen better days and had more stains on it than a butcher's apron, and there was only one wardrobe; the rest of the room was void of furniture.

BJ sat on the bed and pulled from beneath his mattress a bag containing a spoon, syringe and leather tourniquet. I then realised that he was either taking his works with him or he was going to hit up. Much to my distaste he asked me to tie the tourniquet round his arm as he was having problems injecting. Most drug abusers' veins eventually collapse after constant injections of heroin and BJ fitted that bill. I tied the tourniquet tight around his left arm while he one-handedly prepared the heroin; the syringe was quarter full. He then proceeded to remove the air from the syringe, placed the needle into a small vein in his left arm and injected.

This was the first time in my police experience I had ever actually witnessed and assisted a drug abuser feeding the habit. BJ's eyes changed instantly from clear to glazed; the rush must have hit his body at a thousand miles per hour. As I looked down I watched the syringe fill with blood. I had to draw his attention to it. BJ was dazed. He removed the syringe from his arm and placed it in his mouth, injecting the blood straight down the back of his throat. I felt my stomach heave.

I had other things to worry about, though – one was that he did not OD (overdose) while I was with him. I released the tourniquet and BJ fell back on to the bed. He just lay staring at the ceiling. I took the opportunity to give his flat a quick turn over to see if there was anything that shouldn't have been in it. I moved into the kitchen and then made the same check of the toilet. On my return BJ was sitting on the edge of his bed with his head in his hands. He looked up and smiled – he was coming back to earth.

A few minutes later BJ was sitting in the front seat of my car as if nothing had happened. I drove back to Croft Road and Vinnie came down and joined us. I introduced Vinnie to BJ; they got on like a house on fire. BJ directed us to a council estate where we drove into Hambledon Street on the other side of the town centre. Hambledon Street was exactly like the houses drawn by the painter Lowry, the only things that were missing were the matchstick cats and dogs. BJ told me to stop directly outside a bright blue door. BJ got out of the car, followed closely by Vinnie. After a few loud knocks the upstairs window was thrown open and a 19-year-old female looked out. On seeing BJ she came downstairs and opened the door. BJ and Vinnie disappeared into the void.

A short time later both came from the house. Vinnie was smiling from ear to ear – he had scored. BJ returned to the front seat and Vinnie sat in the back. I met Vinnie's eye in the rear-view mirror and he winked, giving me the nod that he was now in possession of heroin. While en route to our own area, BJ openly admitted that he had been responsible for robbing an elderly woman at the local church coffee morning and that he had stolen a cash box containing a small amount of loose change.

Vinnie and I dropped BJ off in the town centre and drove back to our flat to inform the inquiry team that we now had heroin in our possession. Vinnie was excited and rightly so: he had also walked into a lion's den, although his safety net had been outside in the Ford Granada. We contacted Ben's office and arranged to meet Neil and Peter in the car park in Seaton Sluice later that day. Vinnie made up his notebook and we concealed the items within the flat.

I drove alone to Jay Falmer's. I was uncomfortable introducing Vinnie to Jay, considering his fiery temper with strangers. I was welcomed into Jay's house with open arms and he sold me another two deals and invited me back later that day to join him in smoking a joint. This was to be one of the occupational hazards of the job whilst dealing with so many drug abusers. I had made the decision that if I was pushed to smoke cannabis I would refuse, saying I had business to conduct later that day and I wanted to keep a clear head – it worked every time.

I offered Jay Falmer some of the jumpers at a knock-down price. He was touched by the fact that I had included him in the scam. I said that I would drop off some jumpers later and possibly bring my brother with me and introduce him. Jay said that was no problem.

Later that day Vinnie and I returned to Jay's house carrying half a dozen Pringle jumpers. I told him I would collect the money at a later date as a sign of trust. During this operation we had to be careful that we did not buy too many drugs in the one day since Blyth, for want of a better description, was a small village as opposed to a town and all the drug dealers and abusers knew each other. If the two Scots guys were entering and exiting houses on an hourly basis, word could get round or we could be seen; we had to tread warily.

At this juncture I decided to take Vinnie around and introduce him to Anne and Wayne. I felt they both took to Vinnie better than they had taken to me, possibly because I always had a clear head and as far as they were concerned Vinnie was one of them: a drug abuser. Vinnie fitted in well with them, which I was pleased with. We sat talking in Anne and Wayne's house for hours. They were actually an interesting couple. Anne was older than Wayne and had been a good-looking woman in her day but the signs of drug abuse were now beginning to tell on her face and her complexion. Wayne, who had suffered from polio as a kid, was thin and wiry. He walked with a limp, which surprised me considering he was a cat burglar. There wasn't much they didn't disclose to us, all of which was passed on to criminal intelligence.

Over the next few days Vinnie and I were to continue purchasing drugs from the girl in Hambledon Street and, on the odd occasion, from Anne and Wayne.

Time was flying on. Two days had passed with Vinnie and it was now time for him to return to his own force. It is a true saying that you do not know people until you have actually lived with them. Vinnie was a smoker and had different habits from myself. Where I would be washing, dusting and vacuuming to keep the flat clean, he would leave everything at his backside; sometimes I thought he did it to wind me up and, if so, he succeeded.

Prior to Vinnie leaving we had to spend half a day at the safe house. This job wasn't just about making drug deals, the 'i's had to be dotted and the 't's had to be crossed for the paperwork. Notebook procedure was a crucial part of police evidence when presenting a case for the Crown. Ben's team were methodical. They would check everything once, twice and then, for safety, a third time. All the targets we dealt with had their own personal files which would contain the exhibits and any video footage or taped conversations, all of which had to be transcribed prior to any arrest being made at a later date. My handlers John and Ben had decided that if and when the operation concluded, the flat would be cleaned, meaning all the technical equipment would be removed, and possibly three weeks later Ben would organise the hits on the addresses where the targets resided. This would be done in the early hours of the morning. However, all that was some time away.

Vinnie, Ben and the team left and I was once more alone in the safe house. I decided I was not returning to Blyth. I had a long, hot shower and lay on top of the bed in the cottage. I awakened seven hours later but my body was still tired. That weekend, when I came home, Wendy and my girls commented that they thought I was changing. On the Saturday night Wendy and I sat having a quiet drink together and she said that I was becoming very withdrawn, certainly not my usual jovial self. I explained that I had a lot on my mind and that the operation meant everything to me. At this time I didn't realise that my personality was changing slightly and it was due to the stress and pressures I had been under.

The following Monday morning I decided to call in to see my colleagues at the squad. It was good to see the guys, who I hadn't caught up with for many weeks. Police officers have a great sense of humour that acts as a form of escapism when there is a need to release pressure. Nearly everybody I spoke to commented on my weight increase and that wherever I was working I was obviously getting fed too well. Unknown to them, the weight that I was putting on was due to the excessive alcohol I was consuming while trying to identify new targets. I felt awkward when my colleagues asked where exactly I was working. They should have known better than to ask. How could I give them an honest answer? However, I didn't want to appear to be a prima donna. I changed the location to Birmingham and told them some of the stories, changing the characters' names and locations. I made up stories, which I'm sure they were aware were fictitious, to give them a laugh.

By Monday evening I was buried back in my routine in Blyth. It was a strange feeling as I stepped through the front door of my flat; everything was so familiar to me. That night, when I lay in bed, I thought of my weekend break and of what Wendy had said about how my personality was changing. I put it down to being tired.

The following morning I received my early-morning phone call from Ben. 'What are you like?' This was his standard opening gambit.

'As fit as a butcher's dog,' I replied.

I was getting to know Ben well and in fact had been introduced to some of his family. That day Ben didn't sound his usual self. I had known Ben long enough to sense that there was something wrong and knew he wouldn't take objection if I challenged him on it.

Ben was his usual diplomatic self and said, 'It's nothing to worry about. It'll be sorted.'

I asked him to explain further. Ben told me in confidence that he was having differences with a senior officer within his force and as such the senior officer intended moving Ben away from the operation – this would mean a new operational head and possibly a change in tactics. This again was to be another setback for Operation Claymore.

I asked Ben what the implications would be. He paused and said it would mean possibly shutting the job down for a week or two. I began to lose it and reminded Ben that we had enough cover stories going, without complicating matters and disappearing for two weeks. It was now the middle of November and getting close to Christmas. Ben said that he was having a meeting later that day with his senior officer to discuss the circumstances and he would call me back.

Yet again I was alone with nobody to bounce things off. I decided that I was not in the frame of mind to deal with some of the targets and therefore decided I would go to the local swimming baths and enjoy some leisure time.

I returned to the flat late morning and contacted Ben, who informed me the news was not good: he had officially been removed from Operation Claymore. I immediately contacted John, my handler, and asked for further instructions. I was told to shut down the flat and remove my belongings from both the flat and the safe house and return to Scotland. I took it upon myself to provide some sort of explanation to the targets. I called round their various abodes and told them that I had to return to Scotland due to a family bereavement. At least now I could return to Blyth should the operation continue without having to make any more excuses.

The following day I reported for duty as usual at the Crime Squad. My routine changed somewhat from that in Blyth. I was back in the crew room, laughing and joking with the guys, but I found it hard to readjust. Within an hour of returning to the Crime Squad I was back out on mobile surveillance, from one extreme to the next. The first day back in the squad was long, my mind was on other things and I was still returning back to earth after being on a high for so long in the Blyth area. The following day, John, my handler, had advised me that Ben had approached the Assistant Chief Constable within his area and that discussions were ongoing as we spoke. John was confident that the decision to remove Ben would be overruled by the ACC and that Operation Claymore would take off again.

The following week, Operation Claymore was back on and it was all hands on deck. I met Ben at the safe house on the Monday morning and he filled me in on exactly what had happened. He had clashed with his superintendent who decided to clip Ben's wings by removing him from Operation Claymore. The Superintendent obviously did not understand the work involved in setting up the operation and as such the ACC had overruled his decision and Ben was now back at the helm. The operation had now been running for almost two months and both Ben and I decided that we would step up a gear and start being slightly more aggressive in our attack. Prior to leaving the safe house, Ben informed me that the Blyth Valley Member of Parliament, Ronnie Campbell, had stood up some weeks earlier in the House of Commons and complained of the drugs problem within Blyth. It was now in the public eye that something had to be done in the area. Unknown to Ben and me – and the Honourable MP Ronnie Campbell – the MP's brother would soon fall victim of Operation Claymore.

14

THE MP'S BROTHER

WINTER WAS NOW setting in and Blyth became an even colder place where the wind was chilling and the nights were cold and damp. Since returning I had been floating in and out of the targets I had already made, just to keep their acquaintance and keep them on the boil. I had scored a few more deals from Begsie. He was now calling round to the flat on a regular basis, unwittingly volunteering good criminal intelligence that was recorded live on camera.

BJ was looking worse for the weather. He was now on a methadone course (the prescribed substitute for heroin) which should in fact have weaned him off heroin but he was still using heroin on top of the methadone. There was a saying in the Gorbals when I was a young lad. I remember the adults saying it when somebody was near death's door: 'You can smell the clay off him', which in laymen's terms meant he was ready for the ground very shortly. I could smell the clay from BJ.

By now my face was well known within the local hostelries and during my visit to one such spot I befriended a woman by the name of Lucy. Lucy's ex-husband was inside and she never revealed what he'd done. I had managed to build a rapport with Lucy and her son Billy – a small player who dabbled in the drug scene. During my time in Lucy and Billy's company I declared that I smoked cannabis.

One evening, alone in the pub with Billy, I mentioned that I was trying to score some cannabis but my dealer was out of town. Billy volunteered to introduce me to a friend who could possibly help me out. Billy and I left the pub and directed by him I drove a short distance out of the centre of Blyth. En route Billy joked and said the guy we were going to score from was a heavy, a real heavy. Billy laughed nervously. He said that this dealer was called John and that he was a bit rough around the edges. He warned me that John could be violent. I joked and said, 'You haven't met Jay Falmer.' Billy told me Falmer was a pussycat compared to John.

As we approached our destination Billy got cold feet and said that he would go into the house alone. I was not in a position to argue. He got out of the car and went into a semi-detached council house in a decent residential area. Fifteen minutes passed before he came to the door and called me in. I got out of the car and went to the front door where I was introduced to a lad called Mattie. Billy had referenced me and Mattie asked what I was looking for. I placed the order and Mattie disappeared from the hallway into the living room area. I heard voices and then Mattie returned with my piece of cannabis. We exchanged pleasantries, shook hands and Billy and I left.

During the drive back, Billy was like an excited young kid having introduced me to such a big player. I couldn't understand why Billy was in such a state. He laughed and proceeded to tell me the tale.

Mattie was a runner for the main player, John – a local worthy who had served time in prison. I told Billy that didn't impress me.

Billy replied, 'John's surname is Campbell.'

This meant nothing to me at this point so I asked him to explain.

Billy said, 'John Campbell has a brother who is an MP called Ronnie Campbell.'

The penny dropped. I had an immediate rush of adrenaline. What a scoop! Blyth MP standing in Parliament, complaining about the drug problems in Blyth, when in fact his own brother was a dealer. This was not a reflection on the MP's own character, however. It is an old saying that 'You can pick your friends but you can't pick your family' and we should never tar everybody with the same brush.

I was wound up and could not wait to contact Ben and inform him of our possible next target. I dropped off Billy at the pub and made my excuses to leave. I returned to the flat and phoned Ben. He could hear the excitement in my voice and when I told him who my next target could be, he said, 'You're as fit as a butcher's dog.' We both laughed. Ben suggested that I attend the Waterloo Bar and buy myself a 12-year-old malt – I had certainly earned one.

Operation Claymore was back on-line, full steam ahead.

After completing the necessary paperwork, contacting my handler and going through the long process of exchanging notebooks and exhibits I returned to the Waterloo Bar to take Ben up on his offer. While standing at the bar awaiting the arrival of my 12-year-old malt I had a quiet laugh to myself. Unknown to me this was seen by Nigel, my upstairs neighbour. Nigel joined me and, on seeing the whisky, asked what the special occasion was. With my tongue in cheek I told him I had received some good news and that things were looking up. Nigel did not pursue the matter. After a few beers we became more relaxed than usual. He told me he had been in the army, prior to becoming a gas fitter. I then told Nigel that I had not always been a lorry driver. I said that I had dabbled in this and that and had contacts throughout the country; I said that I never stayed in the same place too long as things had a habit of catching up with you. Nigel understood where I was coming from.

The conversation eventually came round to the Waterloo being a very successful pub. Unintentionally, I threw in a one-liner saying, 'If this place was to be robbed the takings would no doubt be high.' It was meant as a genuine conversation piece. However, Nigel went further and proceeded to tell me what nights the best takings were made. Nigel explained that he was friendly with the manageress and that he knew when the most money would be available for the taking. I could not believe what I was hearing. I had picked this place as my local social pub, a place for me to chill out, but all of a sudden I was being given the opportunity to rob it.

I told Nigel that this was not my scene and that the pub was dodgy, hoping that he would back off. Nigel told me that this was not the time and the place to discuss something like this and if I was interested I should speak to him outside the pub. I agreed and we moved on with our conversation.

The 7.30 a.m. call arrived and as usual I was 'fit'. I proceeded to tell Ben of the circumstances surrounding the aftermath of my 12-year-old malt. Ben said that he would prefer it if another undercover was to deal with Nigel as I was concentrating on infiltrating other targets. Nigel was too close, given the location of his abode. As it was I was anonymous and could move freely about the flat without Nigel becoming suspicious. I agreed and as such Ben contacted SO10 and arrangements were made for a further two undercovers to be brought into the body of the operation with a view to them dealing with Nigel.

I had no further communication with Nigel for over a week but then made it my duty to seek him out in the Waterloo. I approached Nigel and reminded him of our previous conversation and asked if he was still interested. Nigel was more than willing and said that he would call round to my flat in the next couple of days. I told him that I had two mates coming up from London and it would be better that a couple of Londoners do the job rather than me as my accent was too noticeable and that these guys were not known in Blyth. Nigel smiled, raised his glass and replied, 'Cheers.'

That evening I decided I would attempt to approach Mattie on my own with a view to getting an introduction to the infamous John Campbell. I drove to John Campbell's home address and knocked on the door.

I was met by Mattie who at first was unsure as to who I was. I explained the whole story – who had introduced me and so on – and was invited in. Without any thought or hesitation I was led into the living room where I saw Campbell seated in front of a large glowing gas fire. Mattie introduced me to John, who did not flinch from his position. John Campbell made no effort to look at me and I could barely make out his 'hello' through his rough Newcastle voice. Mattie left the room, leaving me a little uncomfortable. I attempted to make brief conversation with Campbell but he showed no interest in my presence.

Mattie returned a few minutes later, empty-handed. My stomach began to churn and I could hear my heartbeat. Was I over-reacting or was I about to leave the house through the front window? Campbell was a very cold man. I could not make out what he was thinking or tell how he felt. I concentrated instead on his gofer, Mattie, who was either high on dope or just thick.

I had been in the house for approximately ten to fifteen minutes and there had been no mention of tack, so I decided to take the bull by the horns and ask Mattie if he could sort me out. Mattie apologised and asked how much I wanted. On this occasion I decided to push my luck and take double what I had the last time. As Mattie and I were exchanging contracts, Campbell asked me where I came from. I quickly proceeded into overdrive and give him my full cover story. Campbell's guard remained firmly in place.

I would have put Campbell in his mid to late 40s. He looked strong and fit. Still, it was difficult to learn more about him because I couldn't get inside his head and he was so unemotional. Having completed my presentation to Campbell I asked how long he had been in Blyth. Campbell told me his story, none of which I could understand. Campbell was totally incoherent to me; his voice was so rough – either through heavy smoking or constant shouting – and this quality was assisted by his heavy Geordie accent.

I felt uncomfortable and I did not know when to reply, 'Oh,' 'Yes,' 'No,' or 'Is that right?' at the appropriate times, so I just remained silent.

When Campbell finished I decided it was time for me to leave. I informed Mattie and Campbell that I had some friends in my flat and that I had been away some time trying to source tack. I asked them to excuse me and said I would catch up with them later. Campbell turned and looked at me straight in the eye, smiled and said something. Mattie showed me the door and I left.

I immediately returned to the flat and removed my technical equipment. I checked that everything was working and that I had got Campbell's comments on tape, hoping that the inquiry team would be able to decipher his accent. I contacted the team, completed my notebook and thereafter attended the prearranged meeting with Neil or Peter. John Campbell was eventually sentenced to four years in prison for supplying drugs and assaulting a policeman.

Over the next week or so I continued to service the targets. We had decided that the original plan was to score a few deals and then move on, although I felt slightly uncomfortable with this. I had to walk or drive around Blyth and should I per chance meet one of the targets there would be questions asked as to where I had been and why I had not been back for some more kit. It was decided we would visit those targets previously bagged at least once a fortnight. Billy and Lucy had taken me into their confidence and I was now getting good-quality intelligence from them in respect of some of the major players in the Blyth area. Lucy knew everyone in the Blyth area and was a good contact to have.

I had been given the names of some other dealers and had been shown their addresses by BJ. It was my intention to try some cold calls and see if I was successful. I now had plenty of names that I could use to reference me over the door, should my credibility or identity be challenged.

One of the houses pointed out to me by BJ was situated in Disraeli Street, a street I visited on numerous occasions to buy cannabis, but this particular door was a heroin dealer's. I decided that I would chance my luck. I parked the car a short distance away and proceeded to walk towards the door. BJ had told me that the householder was a guy by the name of Jock.

I knocked on the door and a woman answered. Briefly I told her my name and that a friend had said I could score some good gear. The woman took one look at me and told me to fuck off or she would phone the police. She was either suspicious of me or I had chosen the wrong door. I decided to back off and take observations from nearby. After about four or five minutes I saw a known junkie walking past me on the other side of the street. I moved into police-surveillance mode and followed him on foot. The guy, a heroin user, passed the front door and walked on. He continued to the end of the terraced houses, turned left and then left again into the lane. Following at a discreet distance I observed the junkie turn into the backyard of the house next door to the one I had been trying to score from. I could feel my cheeks flush with embarrassment at having gone to an innocent party's door and trying to score. No wonder the woman told me to fuck off.

Within minutes the guy reappeared, no doubt having achieved his objective. I took a long deep breath and retraced his steps into the back yard. On entering the yard it was like walking into the set of *Coronation Street*. I half expected Ken Barlow to open the back door when I knocked on it. After a few knocks the door was opened by a male in his 40s wearing oil-stained denims and a motorbike jacket. He was thinning on top with hair tied in a bow flowing down his back. I immediately kicked into my script and introduced myself. I informed him that a friend, BJ, had said that he was okay to score off. The guy was hesitant and replied in a broad Scottish accent, 'I don't know you from fuckin Adam.'

I joked and said 'No, my name's not Adam, I'm Dave. I know you've never seen me before but I've been in Blyth for six months.'

I proceeded to rhyme off some of the names I had been scoring from already. Making the excuse that I had been to a few of their houses and they had no gear left and that they had suggested I come to him, I felt my mouth drying up and I was struggling for saliva. There was a deathly silence and then Jock invited me in.

As I entered the small kitchen area I heard a loud clatter and bang at my back. I immediately swung round only to see Jock pushing an old Norton motorbike across the back door, preventing my exit and preventing entry. My first instinct was to rush forward and push him out of the way. I was fearing for my safety. I realised that it was a delay tactic should the drug squad come through the back door; it was normal practice for most drug dealers either to have a secure metal framework with bolts and sliding bolts or alternatively barricade the door – in this case with an old motorbike. Jock led me into the living room area where I saw a three-year-old child playing in the corner with her toys. He asked me exactly what I was looking for and I told him I wanted to score. He then left the room and proceeded upstairs. A few moments later he had me sorted and I was on my merry way. In the short time that I had been with Jock I learnt that he had come from an island on the west coast of Scotland. My confidence was on an all-time high and I returned to the flat to go through the daily routine of completing notebook and exhibits. I contacted the handlers and later met them at the usual place.

The next day I was joined by Vinnie, who was looking after the flat for me while I returned home to see my family. I was slightly nervous at leaving

Vinnie as he was over keen and ambitious to leave his mark on the job. Vinnie had decided that he would play with Anne and Wayne and try and obtain more contacts through them. Vinnie, for some reason, had taken a personal dislike to Paul in the second-hand shop, which was unfortunate because when playing the role as an undercover you cannot let your personal feelings or thoughts in respect to an individual affect the operation. Vinnie drove me to the safe house where I showered and changed into my own personal effects and headed north.

As I got closer to Scotland I could feel myself coming down off the high and I began to feel very tired. Prior to returning home I called into my own local hostelry where I recharged my batteries with three or four vodkas. My mood and self-esteem began to come back up.

Over the weekend I continued to unconsciously recharge my batteries by pouring myself a large vodka or whisky. I was unaware that this was an unnatural routine for me as I had been living this way for the last two and a half months. Wendy pointed out that I was still in working mode, chewing gum and spitting when I was out with her and the girls. She told me on numerous occasions to step out of my role – I was now the family man – and this caused many arguments. I was now feeling glad at the thought of heading back to Operation Claymore.

On the Sunday afternoon before leaving home my father mentioned to me that he had noticed a change in my personality and was concerned that I was working long hours. I had not fully explained to him the type of work I was doing because he would have been worried sick. My father thought I was on long-term surveillance on a major operation in England.

While driving back to Newcastle on the Sunday evening I reflected on my weekend off. I had begun to notice that my tolerance for my loved ones was strained. I put this down to the long hours and tried every excuse that I possibly could to remove the guilty feeling from my shoulders.

On Sunday evening I met up with Vinnie at the safe house and he informed me of his weekend work. Vinnie had continued to score from Anne and Wayne and on a couple of occasions had purchased jewellery and other proceeds stolen from burglaries in the Blyth area. Vinnie had also scored from a couple of new heroin dealers whom he had been introduced to by Anne and Wayne; all in all the targets were mounting. On Monday morning Vinnie left Blyth and headed home.

That morning I received a telephone call from Ben to say that a senior officer from SO10 was travelling to Newcastle to observe how Operation Claymore was going. Ben had suggested that the senior officer, who was in fact an experienced undercover himself, come into Blyth and see the operation first hand. I agreed and felt honoured that someone with such experience would spend the time to come north and visit us.

Early lunchtime I met Ben at the Holiday Inn in Newcastle, along with Steve – the experienced UC from SO10. Ben had briefed Steve on exactly how the operation was going and Steve, being the usual professional, showered me with praise, a tactic used to increase confidence in young undercovers. Steve was playing the game and I followed suit, I took Steve to the flat and showed him the technical. As we were leaving the flat to give Steve the grand tour I was pleasantly surprised by an unscheduled visit from Popeye.

Steve and I were driving away from the flat when Popeye waved us down. I told Steve we were going live and that he was now going to be an official part of Operation Claymore. With a flick of the switch my vehicle was now a recording studio. I pulled over to the kerb and stopped and, as if on cue, Steve rolled down his window.

Popeye stuck his head into the car. He asked why I had not been round to see him over the last couple of weeks and why I had stopped training. I told Popeye I had been unwell and I would explain to him later. Popeye told me that he owed me money for the jumpers and booze and asked if I would call round and see him. I introduced him to my mate Steve who stepped into the role immediately. After a few minutes we drove off.

I spent the rest of the afternoon showing Steve around. Early on I took him into one of my local pubs where we met up with Billy and Lucy and later that evening I met up with them again. Lucy showed particular interest in Steve but by the evening Steve was sitting in the Holiday Inn contemplating whether to have white or red. I told Lucy that Steve was a major player in London and that he was heavily into distribution of heroin and cocaine. I also beefed Steve's CV, saying that he was considering sending gear from London up to Blyth; this was just another part of my cover story, told with a view to increasing my credibility. Lucy seemed very interested in Steve's line of business. I told her that Steve and I had been involved in the past and that we had conducted some tasty transactions over the years. Lucy was now stepping up a gear and showing her true colours, divulging certain information about the major heroin suppliers in the Blyth area. I reciprocated and informed her I was in fact an armed robber, now in retirement. I intimated to her that after the new year it was my intention to move down to London and come out of retirement. I said to Lucy and Billy that I required some tools for the job and as such would be moving to other parts of the country to purchase the necessary equipment.

It was now early December and the Christmas spirit was in Blyth. Lights and decorations were everywhere except in the undercover flat. Whilst the normal people of Blyth went about buying Christmas paper and presents for family and friends I was still sniffing about trying to get new targets. Slowly but surely I felt my head going down as I thought of my colleagues in the squad arranging their Christmas nights out. My family and friends were out buying Christmas presents, while I was still trying to weed out the drug dealers of Blyth. Unfortunately, the type of people I was dealing with did not celebrate Christmas in the usual family way to which I had been accustomed. I had at one point thought of buying a Christmas tree for the flat but this would have been out of character for the Scottish hard-man dealing in drugs.

The nights were getting lonelier and the days were becoming longer. Unconsciously my alcohol intake was increasing. I felt myself going down with the mood swings. To compensate I would top myself up with the odd whisky or vodka but I was keeping my head clear and still conducting the business with the contacts I had made in Blyth. Lying in bed at night was the hardest time. I would switch from Blyth to what I would normally be doing in December back home in Scotland. I was phoning Wendy more often to try and get the buzz and received the Christmas spirit from the family, sent down the telephone line.

The only consolation was that the operation was going well, better than we had anticipated. I found myself slipping off more and more to the safe house during the day to chill out and try and get back into the David Corbett I once was. I was pulling together more meetings with the inquiry team and using every excuse under the sun to have a quick get-together at the safe house. It was a lonely time.

15

ANT AND DEC

THE TWO LONDON undercovers had arrived and Ben had them at the safe house. Ant and Dec – as I nicknamed them because of their uncanny likeness to the young Geordie TV presenters – could have sold sand to the Arabs; they knew their craft well and were a pair of London chancers. The boys specialised in arranging and setting up armed robberies. They were a good choice so once again I followed the normal routine of briefing the guys while en route back to Blyth. That night I took Ant and Dec with me to the Waterloo for a social drink, hoping we would meet up with Nigel; luck was not on our side and Nigel was nowhere to be found. We returned to the flat with a carry-out meal and spent the rest of the evening exchanging undercover stories.

In the morning I tracked down Nigel and arrangements were made for him to call at the flat later that afternoon. On cue, Nigel appeared and was introduced to the two likely lads from London. Nigel painted a picture of how they could turn over the owner of the Waterloo Bar. Nigel, being the professional, even obliged by drawing plans of the layout of both the pub and the owner's home; the whole proceedings were caught on camera and the job was done and dusted. I took a back seat and left it to the London boys.

Later that night we arranged a meeting at the safe house where Ant and Dec were debriefed by Ben. Notebooks were completed and evidence handed over.

When the work was done I travelled with the London boys to the holiday resort of Whitley Bay where we unwound, had a few sherries and toured the nightlife. The following morning I dropped the lads off at Newcastle Central station where we said our farewells.

Back at Blyth I paid a visit to Popeye's gym where I made my apologies for not calling and seeing him sooner. Popeye showed genuine interest as to why I had been evading him. I told him it was a long story, embarrassing actually, and that I did not want him to think any less of me. Popeye fell for my story of woe and invited me into his parlour, where for the first time I saw the two kestrels perched in the corner. I was aware that it was only the chosen few that Popeye invited into the small office where he could talk out of sight of his regular customers.

I then proceeded to spin Popeye a yarn. I told him I had been to a rave in Scotland where I had dropped a couple of Ecstasy tablets. The following morning I awoke to find that my nervous system had been affected by what I had taken the previous evening. Popeye asked me to describe what kind of Ecstasy I had swallowed and I painted a false picture for him. Popeye did not appear surprised or disappointed in my actions and much to my surprise asked why I had not come to him for Ecstasy. I tried very hard to hide my surprise but eventually blurted out, 'I didn't know you dealt in the fucking stuff.' Popeye told me it was only people he trusted that he would supply. I was now one of Popeye's trusted customers. I took this opportunity to tell Popeye that I was attending a rave the following weekend in Edinburgh and it would be ideal to take a couple of Ecstasy tabs up with me. Popeye asked how many I was looking for and I told him, 'Just a couple for me and my mate.' I didn't want to appear too ambitious by going in with a heavy order. He told me to come in and see him the day prior to the rave and he would get me sorted. He then paid the monies owed to me for the jumpers and whisky.

Returning to the flat I could hardly contain my excitement. I had just bagged a target that the drug squad and crime squad had previously been unable to reach. I called Ben who went silent and then retorted, 'What are you like?' to which I made my usual reply. Ben then told me that some days earlier Wayne had been arrested for attempted fraud in the Newcastle area and was presently on remand in Durham prison. Armed with this information, my next port of call was a social visit to Anne and Wayne's house. Anne was not at home, but young Scott gave me the news and stated that his mother had travelled up to Durham prison to see Wayne. I told Scott to tell his mother to contact me.

Later that evening Anne called round to my flat where live on camera she talked me through the events leading up to Wayne's arrest. Anne also told me what line of defence they would take when the trial came to fruition. Unexpectedly she asked if I would be in a position to give her a lift to Durham prison and go in and see Wayne with her. I had to quickly think on my feet – the last place I wanted to show my face would have been in Durham prison, just on the off chance that someone there could possibly identify me as being a police officer. I told Anne I had no objections taking her down to the prison but felt more comfortable staying on the other side of the wall. She understood. Arrangements were made for me to meet her and Scott and drive them through to Durham the following day. I informed Ben of my proposed journey and that I intended to spend some social time in Durham and thereafter bring Anne back to Blyth.

As arranged we met at 1 p.m. and drove to Durham prison. Whilst en route to Durham, Anne informed me that she was going to slip Wayne some gear. I asked her how she would get the gear past the prison officers. 'Easy,' she said, 'I'll conceal it in my tush and once I'm through the search area I'll go into the loo and retrieve it.' This done, she continued, she would place the drugs, which were wrapped in clingfilm, in her mouth and on meeting Wayne she would give him a French kiss and exchange them orally. This was a good scam, which I would pass to Ben for onward transmission to Durham Prison Service when I dropped off Anne and Scott.

The highlight of my journey was when Anne asked me to keep my eyes on the road while she pulled her trousers down and concealed the drugs up her privates. I almost burst out laughing, thinking of the inquiry team, Peter and Neil, reviewing the video evidence in my car and suddenly getting a bird's eye view of Anne's vagina. True to form, Anne pulled her trousers down to her thighs and in full view of the covert camera proceeded to spread her legs and insert the drugs, none of which I saw or wanted to see. I would wait until Neil and Peter gave me a full descriptive rundown of the proceedings back at the safe house.

At Durham prison Anne left the car and said I should return within an hour. I leaned over the driver's seat with a view to opening Scott's door but much to my surprise he had decided he was going into Durham with me. Somehow I needed to get to a telephone without Scott raising the alarm. Whilst driving from Durham prison towards the town centre I took the opportunity to stop the car and enter a local hotel in search of the toilet. I told Scott to stay in the car and, in double time, called Ben and gave him the information. I had been looking forward to having a quiet day in Durham, doing a bit of sightseeing, but young Scott had a different idea. He wanted to go out and commit as much shop-theft as he could within a 45-minute window.

Having parked the car, the first place we headed for was Scott's choice, Woolworths. Scott looked, as I previously mentioned, a lot younger than he was and due to his stature did not draw any attention to himself. Scott headed for the car accessories whilst I made my way to the CD, music and video area. A couple of minutes later I was joined by young Scott who was desperate to leave the store. I asked him if he had been sussed and he informed me, 'No, the fucking thing's heavy.' I looked down and saw that his jacket had been fully zipped up and that there was a bulge protruding from his navel area. We quickly left Woolworths and stood in a doorway where from underneath the jacket he produced a multipurpose cleaning kit for a car, along with four large bottles of coloured T-cut. From his jacket pocket he produced a large carrier bag into which he placed the items before handing the bag to me. Within 30 minutes Scott had obtained approximately £200 in stolen items from various shops within a 100-yard radius.

Fully laden with stolen property we returned to my car and drove back to the prison. Approximately three hours had passed since we dropped Anne off but there was no sign of her. Time was ticking and Scott asked if I would go inside and ascertain where she was. I declined, telling him I had a fear of enclosed spaces.

At approximately 5.15 p.m. – some four hours later – Anne emerged from the public entrance to HMP Durham, her face ashen and drawn. Once in the car she proceeded to explain that initially all had gone well. She had managed to pass the drugs to Wayne via the French kiss but seconds later both she and Wayne had been pounced on by the prison officers. They dragged Wayne away shouting and screaming. Anne was then detained and placed in a side room where she was interviewed. A statement was noted from Anne and drugs were recovered from Wayne's mouth. Due to insufficient video footage no charges were preferred against Anne. However, Wayne would be further charged with having been found in possession of a controlled drug and with an offence against the prison-service regulations. Anne continued to babble on whilst I switched into thinking mode, wondering why Anne had not been arrested. The only conclusion that I could draw was that Ben had asked the prison officers to let her run and just proceed against Wayne. My suspicions were confirmed when I spoke to Ben later that evening. Ben thought it would be better for the operation if Anne was still out and about rather than having her banged up.

It was now two weeks until Christmas and I was still not in the Christmas spirit. My colleagues in the squad were preparing for their Christmas night out, which I of course would not be attending. Some of my targets were also talking about their arrangements for the festive season. When speaking to Wendy she would tell me about the presents she had bought for the family and would ask for my input and thoughts about Christmas Day. I selfishly reminded her that I was not in a position to think of such things until I had returned home.

Meanwhile bad news had come from the inquiry team. Ben had informed me there had been some sort of technical fault with the equipment in the flat and that the job previously discussed with Nigel and the two London undercovers had not been recorded. Ben suggested that we try and get Nigel back into the flat and go over the story with him again. I was aware that we would have to re-enact our ploy with Nigel but at this present time I did not know how.

The weather conditions had changed as we moved deeper into winter. The temperature in Blyth had dropped drastically while torrential rain and high winds were battering Scotland. It was at this juncture of the inquiry that I realised the police service were not as caring as they would have people believe.

I had occasion to phone Wendy at her office one morning only to find that she had not reported for work but instead had phoned to say there had been some domestic problem. I felt nervous as I dialled our home number from a local call box. Wendy answered the phone out of breath. I asked what the problem was and through tears she told me that on returning from work the previous evening she found that the strong winds had removed the roof of our newly built extension. Wendy informed me that along with our next-door neighbour she had been on the roof most of the evening and early morning, trying to secure the large hole with a lorry tarpaulin. I spent the next half an hour consoling Wendy and reassuring her that I would return home within the next 24 hours.

My second call was to my handler in Scotland. I informed him of our domestic situation. John was sympathetic, however no offer of assistance was forthcoming from him or any of my colleagues within the squad. On attending my first course at SO10 you were reassured by the instructors that the undercover officer's welfare and the welfare of his or her family were paramount to those giving support within the force area. Unfortunately this did not seem to be true in my case.

I then telephoned Ben and told him I would be returning home the following day to attend to domestic problems. Ben was sympathetic and suggested that if I wished to leave sooner then I should do so. The operation was going well and I felt just to drop everything and walk off would be unprofessional, especially since I had matters to attend to. I had Nigel to deal with and of course I had to contact Popeye and place another order with him; there were also the targets I had already identified, who I needed to continue to be involved with.

I began to feel at an all-time low. I hadn't noticed the swelling of my alcohol consumption but I had noticed that my weight had increased by over a stone and I was becoming more lethargic. I sat in the flat looking out the window at the people of Blyth going to and from their homes and conducting their daily routines. Although I had decried Blyth at the beginning of the inquiry, there were some decent people there who were trying to lead good lives.

I reflected and my thoughts became negative. Why was I doing this? Nobody cared. Everybody else round about me would reap success and promotion. The recent event of the roof blowing off at home proved to me that nobody really cared about Dave Corbett and his family. I had been staring into space for over two hours, thinking of my present position, asking myself questions. Should I call it a day? I was tired.

The sound of the telephone ringing immediately brought me back to Blyth and I heard the familiar voice of Ben. Ben's call was to make me feel even more insecure when he proceeded to tell me that the local CID were now asking questions about my identity and reasons for being in Blyth. Ben had told me that an informant was drip-feeding his police handler with information surrounding a Scottish guy who had now moved into the area. Ben had been privy to intelligence reports and felt it was his duty to mark my card that they were beginning to look at me. Between the domestic situation and this information I was not having a good day.

I returned to the kitchen and made a large strong coffee, which I intended to lace with some whisky. The controlled-entry intercom buzzed. At first I thought it would be Begsie calling for a social visit; however, as bad as my day had been this caller was to make it worse. On answering the controlled entry I heard the dulcet tones of Popeye. His voice seemed somewhat urgent and he asked if I would allow him in. My earlier distractions had been placed on hold and I was now suspicious as to why Popeye wished to speak to me inside the flat. I immediately let him in and threw the switch, turning the flat into a live studio, but my instincts told me to be wary of him so I decided to meet him in the common hallway.

As I left the flat I looked over the balcony and saw Popeye ascending the stairs two at a time. Something did not ring true; his body language told me something was wrong. When he was level with me he pointed and, still walking slowly, said, 'I've just heard you're Old Bill.'

His words hit me like a 14-pound hammer in the chest, the words that every undercover officer dreads hearing. Within a millisecond, Wendy, my girls and other family and friends flashed through my mind. I half expected

Popeye to pull a handgun from his pocket and shoot me, my mouth was dry, my head was spinning and my stomach churned. This was not a stage scene at SO10 that you could laugh and joke at your actions and walk away from. This was a major player in Blyth accusing me of being a police officer. I had to play an ace card and so turned the tables; taking a deep breath, straightening my shoulders and expanding my chest I retorted, 'Don't fuck with me, Popeye. I'm having a bad day and fucking comments like that are not funny. What's the fucking score?'

Popeye stopped in his tracks, which gave me time to exhale and draw another deep breath. The question was: had it worked? Popeye laughed. He put out his right hand, wanting to shake.

I took one step back and said, 'Popeye, don't fuck with me. This is not funny.'

He was smart enough to know that I was angry. 'I'm only joking,' he laughed.

I continued with my aggressive approach and said, 'Jokes like that I don't need.'

Popeye went into overdrive and told me that he wanted to be sure that I was OK to deal with. He had got a police-officer friend who attended his gym to check the registration number of my car to see who it belonged to. Popeye excitedly continued, saying that the officer had done the check and been approached by a detective chief inspector (DCI) in the CID. The DCI had told the officer to stay clear of the driver of the vehicle he had checked as he was a known armed robber now residing in the Blyth area.

At this moment I could only think that the vehicle had been checked out by the officer and the car had been tagged. If the car was tagged to Ben and someone used the Police National Computer to check the car then Ben would immediately be informed by DVLC in Swansea who would be able to identify when the car was checked and by whom.

I was later to find out that this was in fact the case. Ben had been alerted by DVLC and had decided to approach the officer concerned and ask why my vehicle had been checked. The officer, thinking he had been caught out, explained that he had on a particular date seen a 'heavy' driving the car and thought he would do a check. Ben knew this to be untrue as on the date in question my car had in fact been laid down and I was in Scotland. However, Ben, being the excellent detective he was, decided to add to my credibility by telling this police officer that I was in fact a tasty geezer, a retired armed robber. Ben warned the police officer to stay away from the vehicle and not to communicate this conversation to anyone.

Thereafter the officer had returned and informed Popeye of the details kindly furnished by Ben, which of course further referenced me to Popeye. Popeye laughed at his practical joke, which I still could not find funny. I then proceeded to tell Popeye that the story related was the case and that I did not want it publicly known that I was an ex-armed robber. Popeye seemed impressed and reassured me that it would go no further. Popeye concluded his visit with a further offer of Ecstasy should I need it. He left me standing at the top of the stairs, completely taken aback. I had totally forgotten to invite Popeye in, where I could have had all his comments on camera and audio.

I returned to the flat and poured myself a large whisky. I was shaking uncontrollably – obviously the effects of shock. I replayed Popeye's words in my mind a hundred times, thinking the outcome could have been different if Ben had not been so professional in his approach. Even today I cannot help thinking that if Ben had been a lesser man he may have informed the police officer that the vehicle belonged to an undercover. I have no doubt in my mind that Popeye's visit would have taken a different course. The possible consequences were far reaching and played heavily on my mind. What if Popeye had found out I was UC and passed the information on to others in Blyth? I could have become a target of serious violence so easily whilst I was conducting my daily business, either while entering a house or walking in an alleyway.

I telephoned Ben and informed him of Popeye's visit. Ben remained silent as I babbled on and on, explaining the possible implications the episode could have had for my health and safety. Ben told me to shut up the flat and head to the safe house where he would meet me. I said that there was no need and I couldn't drive anyway as I had consumed nearly a half-bottle of whisky. Ben was obviously concerned for my state of mind and told me he would drive towards Blyth and meet me at a safe distance with a view to taking me to the safe house. I declined and said I would stay inside the flat until my confidence was rebuilt.

I sat alone in the flat for some hours, thinking back to the lecture from the FBI agent at SO10. I knew I was becoming downbeat. I had to pull myself out of this sudden depression and as such I decided to go for a few drinks to the Waterloo and drown my sorrows. In the Waterloo I met Nigel who quietly asked if the London boys were going to do the job shortly. I told him that they were involved in another job in the London area and it would not be until after New Year. The tale was spun to buy some time; I had already decided that some time in January we would invite Nigel back to the flat just to go over the layouts and story prior to Ant and Dec committing the robbery. Nigel and I spent most of the evening together talking about motorbikes and experiences we had shared in our past lives.

The next thing I remember was the sound of my telephone in the flat ringing. I sat up, still fully dressed, realising somehow I had made my way back to the flat. I did not remember leaving the Waterloo or even walking home. I answered the phone. 'What are you like?'

I made my standard reply in a hungover voice.

Ben said he had called me on numerous occasions throughout the night and was slightly worried that I may have gone AWOL. I told Ben I went out for a few drinks and returned and had fallen asleep on top of the bed. Ben suggested that I pack up and head home for a few days to sort out my domestic problems – namely the hole in my roof. I agreed, returning home that afternoon to find Wendy had returned to work and that someone had carried out temporary repairs. I lay on top of my own bed and slept for seven hours.

I was awakened by Wendy sitting at the edge of the bed stroking my forehead. I was completely disorientated, not realising that I was back in my own house. I showered, shaved and Wendy and I went out for a meal. At the end of the evening, Wendy commented that my drinking habits concerned her; she pointed out I had drunk a bottle and a half of wine and consumed enough 12-year-old malt to knock out an elephant for the evening. This caused a heated argument. Wendy went to bed early and I stayed up with a friend, Mr Glenfiddich, in front of a midnight movie.

I heard the noise of the toilet flushing and the electric shower being switched on. I sat forward and looked at the clock on the mantelpiece only to find I had slept all night on the living-room chair. Wendy passed through the living room and told me to go to bed. I knew I had been out of order but Wendy did not appreciate what I had been through in the last few days. Of course, I did not appreciate what she went through every day, worrying about my safety. That evening Wendy returned home and we had a long discussion about Operation Claymore. Wendy was of the opinion that my personality was changing and that I was drinking too much. She advised that I leave the undercover David Corbett in Blyth and return home the family man. I now felt uncomfortable in my own home and was looking forward to returning to Blyth to have the freedom to run my own life again. Looking back I was in fact running away from the truth – the truth being that I had stepped over the fine line in the sand and was now suffering from severe stress.

I remember while attending the SO10 selection course that the emphasis was on stress management. A good undercover officer could identify when he was becoming stressed and with the training could comfortably de-stress himself back to his normal well-being. Unknown to me at this time, I was at the point of no return. I had lost control of my personal stress management, practices and procedures.

16

A BAD CHRISTMAS

PRIOR TO RETURNING to Blyth I met Ben and the inquiry team at the safe house; all three were on good form. We had a quick debrief in respect of the evidence and the targets we had gathered so far. Ben was more than happy with the way things were going, as were Peter and Neil with the evidence. Ben suggested that we work for seven days, closing the inquiry down for a week over the Christmas period. This would give me enough time, hopefully, to get round all the targets and contacts I had made and tell them I was going to Scotland for a break with family and friends.

Ben asked how I was feeling and if my confidence had returned after the recent events. He then told me that an internal investigation into the police officer who had checked my car for Popeye would be conducted at the end of the inquiry. Ben was of the opinion that from now on things would become a little more difficult for me to operate. Apparently there was now more than one informant providing police with information about my movements and activities. I assured Ben that I was back on form and that he had nothing to worry about. Deep down I wasn't so sure. I knew that I was getting tired, although the Christmas break would recharge my batteries and perhaps I could start moving forward in the forthcoming New Year. To lighten the mood Peter and Neil discussed the evidence we had gathered about Anne travelling through to Durham prison. It certainly gave us a few laughs. After spending some time at the cottage with the lads I left Long Framlington feeling better.

Whilst travelling back to Blyth I had occasion to pass a marked traffic-police vehicle which was stationary in a lay-by on the M1 just north of Newcastle. On passing the car I noted I was travelling at 102 mph. Realising the officer may have seen me I immediately reduced my speed to the obligatory 70 mph but it was to no avail. Looking in my rear-view mirror I saw the police vehicle following me with its blue flashing lights and its two-tone siren. I slowed down my speed, hoping the car was after someone else, but it quickly became apparent that I was the target and the officer indicated me to stop. I pulled onto the hard shoulder where I remained within the vehicle. As the police officer got out of his vehicle my mind switched into overdrive yet again. Was this the officer who had checked the vehicle on behalf of Popeye? Or was I about to be charged for speeding? Time would tell.

The officer went to the front passenger-side window, which I put down electronically. He asked if I was the owner of the vehicle and if I was aware of the speed I had been travelling at. I replied 'yes' and 'no,' respectively. The officer then stepped back from the vehicle and conducted an external examination. He checked over all the tyres and finally got his capture of the day: a fraudulent tax disc. He identified that the tax disc was out of date and that it had possibly been altered (this being the tax disc I had purchased from Paul in the second-hand store in Blyth). The officer then opened the driver's door and asked me to accompany him to his vehicle. After noting all my details he informed me that the circumstances would be reported and that I would be summoned to appear at court in the near future. Having asked me if I understood the charges he proceeded to issue me with a HORT 1 form. A HORT 1 is issued by the police when a car is stopped and the driver is asked to produce certain legal documents: MOT certificate, insurance certificate, registration document and driver's licence. I would have to produce my driving licence, MOT and insurance along with registration documents for the vehicle within seven days at an office of my choosing anywhere in the United Kingdom. I informed the officer that I wished to produce at Newcastle police office in the centre of Newcastle. I returned to my vehicle and drove off.

I later communicated to Ben the circumstances surrounding my stop. Ben asked me the road patrol officer's number and informed me that he was not the officer concerned with checking the vehicle on behalf of Popeye. Ben then instructed me at some point over the next couple of days to give the inquiry team the HORT 1 form and Ben would attend to the producing of the said documents.

Once back at the flat I underwent my daily routine of cleaning and making the bed. My blood ran cold when I heard the controlled-entry buzzer. Yet again, I felt my mouth run dry; this was going to be another bottle tester. Panic set in and at one point I considered making an exit through the front window and down the drainpipe into the street. I lifted the controlled-entry handset only to find it was Begsie calling to pay for some of the Pringle jumpers he had taken off my hands. Begsie had been in the flat on a couple of occasions and we had shared a few beers together. I was now getting to the stage of telling him to piss off but couldn't for fear of compromising the job, our friendship and my safety. After a few cans of lager and discussing some of the local worthies in Blyth, Begsie left.

I decided that I would try some cold calls with a view to bagging another couple of targets. One of these cold calls was to be a guy by the name of Lee who stayed approximately a dozen doors away from BJ. BJ had previously pointed this guy's house out but he had never taken me over the threshold. I was now about to try myself. I left the car and walked round to Lee's address, which was a main terraced downstairs council house. On previous occasions, when I had passed in the car, I had observed junkies coming out of the back gate, obviously after having scored. I decided to try the back door. I entered through a blue door which led me into a small backyard. I walked forwards and knocked on the back door, which had a net-curtain on the inside. The net-curtain was pulled over slightly and a man looked out at me. I told him I was looking for Lee and that I wanted to be sorted. He obviously did not know me and without speaking shrugged his shoulders and shook his head as if to say no. I explained that I stayed in Croft Road and that a mate had said it would be OK to call. He was not impressed. The curtain was then drawn over and I was left standing. I about-turned, feeling rejected, and decided to go looking for BJ.

I spent the next couple of hours walking about the centre of Blyth but had no success. I then went to one of the local hostelries where I met Lucy. It was mid afternoon and there was a karaoke about to start. I decided that this would be good-quality time to sit and socialise with Lucy and some of her friends. About 8.30 p.m. I left the karaoke and staggered down to the telephone kiosk near the bus station. I phoned Wendy, who told me that she was not impressed by my actions, meaning I was pissed yet again. I became aggressive and reminded her I was working and it was part of my cover; she reminded me that I appeared to be enjoying it and that she was fed up hearing the same old excuses. In a temper I slammed the phone down and returned to the karaoke, the only place I didn't get asked questions and didn't get any hassle.

I was now enjoying the company of my newly made friends. However, I did remember that I was there to collate and gather as much information as I could. As I laughed and joked with these people, I absorbed every minute bit of information they let slip or volunteered. That information was thereafter transferred to Ben and his team who separated the good from the bad.

The following day I drove round to BJ's address and again went through the daily routine of getting him out of his bed and assisting him to hit up. I told him I was looking for tack and that the sources I had tried had all dried up. BJ, being his usual helpful self, then directed me to an address in Shelly Crescent, a semi-detached council house where the door was opened by a young female with a large Rottweiler by her side. BJ went through the usual introductions and I was invited in. I was taken in to the kitchen area where there were a number of youths in the process of cutting a large slab of cannabis into small pieces. The older male of the team – who appeared to be a bodybuilder and sported a long black ponytail – asked who I was. Without a second thought I gave him my usual introductory CV, dropping every name that knew me in Blyth. The lad appeared impressed and proceeded to sell me another piece of cannabis, saying that I could call back next week if I needed any more.

BJ and I left and while en route back I told BJ that my brother Vinnie was coming and that I really should have got him a score. BJ then took me to an address in Lilac Avenue where he introduced me to a woman called Tracey. Tracey stated that she did not have any gear but could sort us out later that day. Next, BJ took me to an address in Burnside Close where he introduced me to Nicola. I told Nicola that my brother was coming from Scotland and that I needed to score for him. Nicola gladly sold me a deal of heroin. I then returned later to the flat and contacted the inquiry team, informing them that I had another three targets and that more work would require to be done at a later date.

The following day I was joined by Vinnie and we proceeded to further target Tracey, Nicola and the guy with the ponytail and the Rottweilers. Within two days we had secured more evidence and we were back on-line. Vinnie stayed with me for a couple of days and then headed back home to attend social events within his force area.

I had not seen Popeye since his unwelcome visit to the flat. I decided that I would call round and place an order for some more Ecstasy, which I could take home with me to Scotland for the festive season. Popeye was in good form and appeared very comfortable in my company. His conversation was unguarded and at one point I asked him if he would introduce me to his main supplier with a view to me moving Ecstasy north. Popeye volunteered that his contact was a major businessman from the Halifax area and that he doubted very much that the man would meet me as he was suspicious of everyone, thinking they were Old Bill. We both laughed and I placed an order for a small parcel, which I would collect at the end of the week.

Christmas was almost upon us and my final deal before the holidays was to visit Popeye and collect the small parcel. Popeye called me into his makeshift office and proceeded to remove a double electricity socket from the wall. Concealed within the cavity was a cigarette packet from which he pulled out my order for Ecstasy. Ironically he said, 'You never know who's about. That's why I keep my stash in here.' If only he knew.

I paid Popeye for the gear and we shook hands, wishing each other a Merry Christmas. As I was walking down the stairs from Popeye's gym I could not help but think what a shock it would be when he heard the evidence I had stacked against him. I'd have the last laugh.

Later that afternoon I met the inquiry team at the safe house where we completed our notebooks and our exhibit forms. We were all looking forward to our break.

I arrived home two days before Christmas Eve. I had wanted to finish off the Christmas shopping for Wendy and throw myself into the Christmas spirit. However, this was not to be the case. I found it very hard to come back down to earth and be the family man and it was the afternoon of Christmas Eve before I had deleted the images of Blyth from my mind. Wendy was continually hounding me, as were the girls, about the amount of drink I was consuming and the more they drew my attention to my drinking, the more heated the arguments became. Eventually, the night before Christmas, instead of helping Wendy wrap presents, I walked out and went to my local.

For the past ten years it had always been the family tradition to go to the midnight service in the local church. Good times: a small drink before the service and a nightcap before retiring to our beds in anticipation of an early-morning rise to open the presents. This year was to be no exception, except that I returned from the local pub very much under the influence. Wendy and the girls realised something was seriously wrong.

I awoke the following morning with the sound of music coming from the living room and when I looked at the clock I saw that it was 8 a.m. I staggered to my feet and entered the living room to find that the girls and Wendy had started to open their presents. It struck me then that I was slowly moving out of the family circle. The day came and went with no further hitches, however.

On Boxing Day Wendy returned to her work after making it quite clear that she had reached the end of the road. With this veiled ultimatum I pulled myself together and for two days played the game, watching my alcohol intake and acting my old self. The evening before returning to Blyth Wendy commented that she had noticed I was slipping back into the undercover mode. I was beginning to brood, was short tempered with the girls and increasing my alcohol intake.

The following day I left for Blyth, thinking of staying for another couple of days ahead of New Year. On my return I continued targeting those new targets we had identified and servicing the targets we had already made.

Returning to the flat I realised I was not getting the same buzz from the job and Wendy was right: I was changing. I asked Ben to meet me at the safe house as I felt we should discuss the future of Operation Claymore. As I drove to the safe house I reminded myself that it was just a job and that my family meant a lot more to me – and certainly cared a lot more for me – than the police service. The support from my own force over the months had been appalling and to this day I thank God for the commitment shown to me from Ben.

At the safe house I told Ben I was feeling tired and I wanted to know how he felt about bringing Claymore to an end. Ben told me that we had successfully bagged approximately 25 targets and that there was a mammoth task ahead in compiling reports and packages for a full inquiry team. Even so, in his typically frank and honest way, Ben said he would have liked to have continued the job for another couple of months. I asked him to compromise with me and end it at the end of January. Ben agreed somewhat reluctantly.

I returned to Blyth and decided I would try the house in Union Street for Lee. On my second attempt I was met with a blank face peering through the net curtain. Again I explained and pleaded that I was not the plod and for fuck's sake please sort me out. Eventually I embarrassed the face behind the curtain into opening the door and having a conversation. I explained to him that I knew Lee and that my brother was staying with me and was severely strung out. Lee invited me into the kitchen then disappeared into another room, returning with a deal of heroin. Job done. I left and over the course of the next couple of weeks returned on numerous occasions.

Before leaving Blyth to return home to Scotland for the New Year I called in to see Anne and her son Scott. On this occasion Anne was not at home and it was Scott who opened the door. He told me that his mum would be returning shortly and asked if I'd like to come in and wait. I took this as an opportunity to have a go at young Scott and started pumping him for information. During our conversation Scott asked me if Vinnie was still staying in Blyth and from his tone I got the impression that Scott did not like Vinnie. No mistake there, Scott told me, neither he nor his mother liked or trusted Vinnie. This came as a great surprise to me as Vinnie had reported that he had been getting on well with Anne and Wayne. Scott said that his mother got the impression that Vinnie was asking too many questions about too many people in Blyth, and thought that he was possibly a police informant and as such she had decided not to supply him further with heroin. This came as a great surprise to me but it also marked my card not to ask any further questions about their associates.

I later informed Ben of my findings and both of us were of the opinion that Vinnie may have been overzealous on his first undercover job.

On 30 December I went back to Scotland to celebrate the New Year with family and friends. It took me some time to return to being David Corbett, the family man. I was also finding it difficult to sleep and was having the odd occasional flashback of Popeye meeting me on the stairs and the walk down the lonely, dark, damp streets at night.

On 4 January I returned to Blyth knowing that I had only a few weeks to tidy up the targets that we had already identified. Both Ben and I had decided that we would now throw caution to the wind and start approaching those names we had already been given but had not yet bagged. The next two weeks were involved in cold-calling and during such times I had six successful deals, all of which we serviced until the end of the operation.

It was the last week of January. Things began to liven up when I met Lucy in the local hostelry. Lucy by this time had learned that I was not in fact the quiet Scottish lorry driver but a retired armed robber seeking peace and quiet in the Blyth area. Over the past two or three weeks I had drip-fed Lucy that I was moving down to London to commit my final armed robbery that would make me for life. The real move, of course, was my intended moonlight removal from the flat to leave Blyth for good, closely followed by misinformation – spread via Ben's informants – that the Scots lad had been caught doing an armed robbery in London. The Scots lad would be history, until some weeks later when each person who had crossed the path of David Corbett would have their front doors smashed and find themselves arrested for various offences. Only then they would realise that the Scots lad was in fact playing 'both sides of the fence'.

Having planted the seed with Lucy I decided it was now time to tidy up the operation and tie up any loose ends – one of which was Nigel. Ben and the inquiry team had called a meeting at the safe house, thinking of spending a day and a half going over each target and the evidence we had secured. Thereafter we would create a spreadsheet to identify any flaws in the chain of evidence or any further investigation required prior to the operation closing down. At the end of our time at the cottage, Ben decided to call back the two London lads, Ant and Dec, to arrange a second meeting with Nigel; this was arranged for the following Thursday. All in all it appeared we had enough evidence for all the suspects I had been involved with. Ben advised me to start packing what little household items there were in the flat with a view to hiring a van and emptying the flat during the late evening. It was decided that after bagging Nigel on the Thursday evening we would move out.

Over the next week I flitted in and out of all of my targets, obtaining any new references or any fresh intelligence.

Four days prior to the closing of Operation Claymore I happened to meet Lucy in one of the local hostelries. Lucy asked me if I needed any equipment for my job in London. I asked her to explain and she went on to say that she knew of a lad who could supply me with a sawn-off shotgun and ammunition. Not wishing to appear over-keen I said I would get back to her the following day. I contacted Lucy as promised and she arranged a meet at a local pub where she introduced me to the supplier, a guy by the name of Tim. Tim was nervous, as was I, but he agreed to drive me to his house where he would show me the weapon. So Tim, Lucy and I drove to an address on the outskirts of Blyth. Once inside the house we discussed a suitable price and, on coming to an agreement, Tim asked me to accompany him upstairs. Yet again I could hear my heart beat as the adrenaline raced through my body. We entered a rear bedroom which was illuminated by a bare bulb; the room was void of furniture and lying in the corner was a black holdall. The only consolation about the circumstances I was now in was knowing that Tim would be feeling exactly as I felt: nervous, suspicious, uneasy and frightened. His concern would be the danger of me being a cop, while mine was about being ripped off. I'm sure we both wondered if the scenario was a set-up and the danger of being shot was certainly in the forefront of my mind. These questions were bouncing off the four walls of the room.

Eventually Tim knelt down and produced, wrapped in a black polythene bag, a double-barrelled shotgun. Immediately my police firearms training kicked in and I stepped out of the line of fire. Tim handed me the polythene bag and I removed the weapon and made it safe, checking that both barrels were clear. I then asked Tim to produce some ammunition, to which he wisely responded by asking me to place the firearm back in the bag before he showed me the ammunition. Tim may have been apprehensive but he was no fool. I did as requested and then Tim produced from his pockets half a dozen shotgun cartridges. I gave him the sum agreed and, taking the holdall and ammunition, I immediately returned to my car. Back at the flat I contacted the operational team and informed them of the circumstances. A short time later I met with Peter and Neil at our rendezvous point in Seaton Sluice car park. The following morning I received a telephone call from the operational team to say that the evidence obtained during this transaction, i.e. tapes and car video footage, was excellent.

My next task was to contact Nigel to arrange a meeting for the following Thursday. The next evening I called into the Waterloo Bar and spoke to Nigel, who agreed to come to the flat at 5.30 on Thursday evening.

Like all people who have handed in their notice at their place of employment, the longest part of their notice is always the last week. Operation Claymore was proving to be par for the course: the clock seemed to stand still and the days got longer and longer. Throughout the following week I bagged a couple of smaller dealers by purchasing cannabis and amphetamine. I could no longer reach the same adrenaline high previously felt when I was involved in cold calls or entering unknown territories.

The Tuesday and Wednesday prior to our final meeting with Nigel, I began to pack up and move everything into a suitable location in the flat in order to clear the place within one hour. All furniture and kitchen utensils, pots and pans etc., were boxed and placed within the spare bedroom, while the television and three-piece suite remained in the living room. The house was now void of all domestic utensils, everything having been boxed up except for the kettle and toaster. Anyone coming into the flat would think all was in order and no suspicion would be raised.

On the Thursday I collected Ant and Dec from Newcastle Central station and while driving back to the flat in Blyth we discussed how we would handle Nigel and try and get him to reiterate his story from some months earlier. At 5.30 p.m., Nigel called and after exchanging pleasantries proceeded to go over the story and again draw further plans for Ant and Dec.

During the proceedings, one of the London lads asked me to make a coffee. Not until the kettle had fully boiled did I remember that all the kitchen utensils and the coffee were packed away in a box in the spare bedroom. All cupboards in the kitchen were void of their contents. After their second request for coffee I told them to fuck off, we were going to the pub as soon as we had finished. Business concluded, we arranged to see Nigel in the local pub later that evening. Meanwhile, back in the flat, both Londoners requested a cup of Rosie Lee. I then explained about the packing and my inability to provide any form of refreshment. While I found the circumstances quite amusing the Londoners felt I could have compromised the whole operation by being so blasé and unprofessional in clearing away all the props of the job. Looking back at it now they were both right but in my state of mind all I wanted was to get away from Blyth as fast as I possibly could and if it meant packing the flat up the night before then so be it. We completed our notebooks and met up with the inquiry team who had in their possession a 3,500-weight transit van which we would drive back to Blyth to use to empty the contents of the flat. It took Ant, Dec and I approximately 35 minutes to empty the full contents of the flat into the van.

The ironic and sad thing was that while we were upstairs checking that there were no telltale signs of us having been there I returned downstairs to find BJ forcing the padlock off the back of the van and leaning in, attempting to remove a cardboard box. I immediately seized hold of BJ, who didn't know if it was New York or New Year. He was high as a kite and had obviously just hit up. I told him to piss off and fortunately for me he did not put two and two together; he scurried off quickly without asking any questions.

Ant and Dec came down and sat in the van while I had one last look over the flat. I had mixed emotions: part of me was glad to be leaving and another part of me wished I could stay and continue and take Claymore further. However, I knew my health was beginning to suffer and that I needed to get back on to an even keel.

The Londoners were booked into the Holiday Inn and I made my way with the van back to the safe house. At the safe house I ceremoniously removed the leather jacket, shirt, denims and desert boots I had been wearing for the last five months; all items were placed in a black plastic bag, never to be used again. I had a hot shower, shaved and proceeded to put on my own personal belongings and jewellery. I could understand how prisoners feel when they return home after having served a long sentence. It was a good feeling having my own belongings around me and it was even better knowing I would not have to return. I drove to the local pub in Long Framlington where I had my last supper in the area. Returning to the farm I felt myself fill up. I could not understand why I was so emotional. When I called Wendy to tell her I would be home the following day, I broke down and sobbed uncontrollably.

The following morning I cleared the cottage of my personal belongings and met with Ben and the inquiry team at the Holiday Inn. I handed Ben the keys of the undercover vehicle, as well as the keys of the vehicle I had been using while staying at the cottage, the cottage keys and finally the flat keys. This was not to be the last time I would meet Ben as I was returning to Newcastle on the day that the targets were to be arrested. Ben drove me to Newcastle Central station where he shook my hand and thanked me for everything I had done. I in turn thanked Ben for his full support and his friendship throughout the operation.

As I walked towards the station Ben drove slowly past me. He rolled down his window and shouted: 'What are you like?'

I replied instantly: 'As fit as a butcher's dog.' I laughed.

Ben drove off, leaving me with tears running down my face. The Scottish Claymore had struck its last blow.

17

THE LAST DAYS

UNKNOWN TO ME life would never be the same after Operation Claymore, which had one more victim to claim: me. The weeks following the conclusion of the operation were difficult. My mind would return to each target, each hit, replaying in my head every moment like a movie. Unlike the team, Ben and the boys, who now had a mountain of paperwork to get through, I had nothing to keep my mind active other than the re-runs. I hadn't realised just how much Claymore had taken over my existence. I had honestly thought that I would have got my life back at the conclusion of the job. I was very unsettled and experiencing difficulty in sleeping. I couldn't achieve any kind of high, my life was on an even plateau and I craved some sort of excitement.

On returning to the squad I realised that my tolerance for colleagues was at an all-time low. I would observe a supervisor chastising a fellow detective constable for some minor misdemeanour and find it tedious and demeaning. Any directive or chastisement towards myself I dealt with by telling the supervisors to 'get a fucking life', not my normal response and completely out of character. I found myself calling in to a pub at lunchtime and recharging my batteries with either vodka or a large whisky – this would give me the tolerance I needed to see me through the day.

At some point during my absence the crime squad had been working on a major operation. I returned to the squad at the latter stages of the operation. The target was involved in the importation of a substantial amount of heroin and was a well-known player in Glasgow by the name of David Santini whose business was about to come to a short, sharp, swift end. The crime squad had been obtaining intelligence and information for many months and had been conducting surveillance on Santini and his associates.

On the evening of his arrest we had information that Santini was travelling to an address in the Glasgow area and that he would have in his possession multi-kilos of heroin. The address was located within a tenement building but the squad had not yet been able to identify the actual house. To aid identification I was asked if I would position myself as near to, or if possible within, the common close of the tenement to identify the house when Santini arrived.

On the day of the strike I was instructed to make my way to the plot, where I positioned myself in the common close with a bag of electrical tools. I proceeded to remove the electrical junction box and take up the role of an electrician. I was at this location for about 15 minutes when I decided I would inform every householder in the close that I was working and that I might require to cut power to enable me to rectify a fault. This done I didn't know if I had spoken to Santini's associate or not. However, after a further ten minutes I was informed via my radio that the target was a short distance away. Some minutes later Santini and an associate entered the building and passed my position, paying no attention to me at all as I watched them ascend the stairs and enter the flat.

I gave Santini a few minutes and then made my way to the door, identifying the now known address by the nameplate. Having obtained the information required I replaced the electric panel and returned to my vehicle where I transmitted all relevant details to the officer in charge who instructed a fellow colleague to obtain a search warrant for the premises. Once the warrant was obtained the house was searched by the drugs squad where they found a large amount of heroin. Santini was subsequently found guilty at the high court in Glasgow and was sentenced some months later to 15 years' imprisonment.

Following the strike we had our usual debrief where one of my colleagues asked how I had felt being in the close awaiting the arrival of the target. Did my bottle go? Did I get excited? Unfortunately I could not provide my willing listener with the answer he craved – I'd felt no fear nor any high. My adrenaline threshold was obviously a lot higher after my experiences in Blyth.

My sleep pattern had got worse; my alcohol consumption continued to grow. In mid February I received a telephone call from Ben asking me to come back to Newcastle to attend a meeting. The meeting was held at the safe house where, along with Ben and the team, we went over all the evidence, tying up any loose ends before the strikes, which were due in a few weeks' time. Ben informed me that it was his intention to call on approximately 300 officers at 4 or 5 a.m. on a specific date and brief them for the first time on Operation Claymore. At the end of the briefing, each officer would be allocated an evidence package containing the target's full details and a brief summary of the circumstances surrounding that target, along with transcripts of tape-recorded interviews, tapes and video footage. Ben had arranged for Vinnie, John and I to be in a hotel in Newcastle where we could monitor the success as it happened.

Two weeks later I found myself at the Copthorne Hotel in the heart of Newcastle, waiting for the strikes. Ben had planned that the addresses in respect of each individual target would be hit at exactly the same time, causing a chain reaction throughout the Blyth area. By 12 p.m. that day all addresses and targets that I had dealt with had been searched and the householders apprehended. It was a strange feeling to think the people I had befriended were now arrested and being told that it was I who had led to them being caught.

Ben fed back information from the operational room. Apparently most of the targets would not believe they had been betrayed by the Scots guy and only after hearing taped interviews or being shown video footage did they yield, realising that they had been part of a major sting.

That evening, having enjoyed a few celebratory drinks with the rest of the team, I returned to the solitude of my hotel room where I lay awake thinking with mixed emotions of my betrayal of these people. However, I only had to remind myself that those people had been involved in the death of the young kids in Blyth through the misuse of heroin. They were the bad guys and the good guys were the parents living in fear of their kids becoming the next victims of the Devil's powder. The local television network did a short story all about the house searches and the arrests, claiming a victory for morality. It was all very much an anticlimax for me after having spent five months wheeling and dealing, befriending and now betraying these people. I just wanted to get it out of my system and move on with my life.

Some time had passed since the strikes but I still could not adjust to a normal routine. At the beginning of March Wendy and I had a normal run-of-the-mill argument for a married couple except that on this occasion I picked up a chair in the sun lounge and threw it through a double-glazed window. As quickly as my temper had flared up it dissolved. I casually walked past Wendy and poured myself a drink. She begged me to get help, to speak to someone about my moods and alcohol dependence. However, unknown to her, during Operation Claymore I had reluctantly identified that my personality was changing and had on numerous occasions addressed the issue with John, who in turn highlighted the problem to senior management.

It had been SO10's practice that every officer involved in undercover work would be seen by a psychiatrist on a three-month basis for the debriefing purposes. Since undertaking undercover for my Scottish force I had not been afforded this facility. As a result of internal politics The Association of Chief Police Officers (ACPO) could not agree on a suitable candidate for Scottish officers and as such I could not be afforded this service.

After my violent outburst with Wendy I again broached the subject with senior officers in the squad, only to be told that nothing had yet been put in place. As this point I decided to withdraw my services from the undercover network. I contacted SO10 and informed them that, due to lack of support, I was officially withdrawing from the register held in New Scotland Yard. I then compiled a report outlining my dissatisfaction with the lack of support, which I addressed to my supervisors. On receipt of this report I was summoned by the Deputy Commander who requested that I change the wording of my report, which he felt unjustly intimated poor management skills on their part. With some reluctance I diluted the contents, removing the reasons why I felt it necessary to withdraw from the register. However, I left the door open by stating if circumstances surrounding support to undercovers should improve I would be agreeable to returning. Having withdrawn my services I became ostracised – I had gone against the system. The isolation certainly didn't help.

The change in my personality came to a head when one evening I was returning from a social night out with Wendy at the wheel. We were on a dark country road and Wendy was travelling at approximately 50 mph when an impatient driver began to flash his headlights, encouraging her to increase her speed. Wendy didn't flinch but my blood pressure went through the roof. The car eventually overtook, at which point I took control of the headlights of our own vehicle and directed our full beam in its direction. The driver began pumping his brakes, eventually stopping his car. Like a raging bull, I ran from our car towards the offending obstacle. Without thinking, I pulled the driver from his seat and held him over the car bonnet; I was within inches of smashing his face onto the bonnet when I heard a child crying. As quick as my temper had flared it subsided and I returned to my normal placid self. I released the driver from my hold and, on walking past the car, I saw a young child seated on the front seat. I realised just how uncontrollable my temper had become and for the first time since Operation Claymore I had to admit to myself the extent of my problem and how out of control I had become.

The following morning I contacted my doctor and made an emergency appointment. My doctor, on hearing the type of work I had undertaken, immediately made an appointment for me to see a counsellor. Meanwhile I continued with my duties in the squad, finding each day a chore and on most occasions topping myself up with the occasional drink at lunchtime. By this time my father had a quiet word in my ear, telling me that he was concerned for my health. I reassured him that I had now identified that I had psychological problems and was seeing a counsellor.

My days at work were getting longer as my tolerance for my colleagues and my supervisors plummeted to an all-time low. I was not enjoying my time back at the squad and I put this down to my present state of mind. The counsellor, who I'd seen for three sessions, was, with the greatest respect, as useful as a chocolate fire guard. She had never dealt with someone who had undertaken my type of work and most of my session time was spent telling the counsellor about the trials and tribulations of undercover policing; although sympathetic she was obviously out of her league.

In April that year I received an invitation to attend at New Scotland Yard – along with Ben – and lecture to new undercover students on the aspects of a long-term infiltration. The course instructors asked me not to sugarcoat but to paint a true picture, warts and all. I assured him I would do just that.

It was a strange feeling returning to the SO10 course, this time not as a rookie but as an experienced undercover. On the morning of my arrival I was introduced to other invited guests there to lecture on the course. During the coffee break prior to myself and Ben doing our 'stint' I was introduced to an FBI agent who would take stage after Ben and me. We had a brief conversation and I told him about my infiltration into a drugs community in the North East of England. The FBI agent seemed impressed and asked numerous questions about the operation. His attention left me feeling important and slightly flattered that an agent from the FBI should show an interest in an insignificant Scottish detective.

Our time came and Ben and I were on. Ben spoke about the management side of the operation, of the politics he encountered while putting the operation together, as well as incidents from the course of the operation – all of which was news to me. After Ben had painted the picture of how Operation Claymore came to be, I was handed the floor. I talked through the job from day one until the final strikes, on occasions choking on my emotions and struggling for words. My main theme throughout the talk was directed at the supervisors attending this course as observers. I could not emphasise enough the need for continual steady support for the undercover throughout a long-term operation. At the end of the lecture Ben and I received rapturous applause and a barrage of questions.

On return to the coffee room I was approached by the FBI agent, who once again lay praise at the work I had undertaken. Looking back now I know I gloated on his praises but if I had known then what I know now I would have played the whole day differently. I then asked the FBI agent if he was over to tell the story about Marty – the FBI agent who had been shot. To my surprise he said no, that he was here to talk about a job he had been involved in whilst undercover which had made the headlines. Typical Yank, I thought, making mountains out of molehills.

Ten minutes later I was seated in the lecture room along with the undercover students when the Commander of SO10 stood at the podium and proceeded to introduce the FBI agent.

The Commander opened his speech: 'It gives me great pleasure to introduce one of the world's best-known undercover agents, Joe Pestoni. Joe infiltrated the Mafia over a seven-year period in America and attained the highest accolade within that organisation as a made man. You will not know Joe Pestoni as his real name, you will probably know him better as Donnie Brasco.'

At this point I felt my stomach heave and my face go red with embarrassment. I have seen the film *Donnie Brasco*, the lead played by Johnny Depp, co-staring Al Pacino, on at least four occasions and each time I have sat in utter amazement at Brasco's achievements during his seven-year infiltration. This guy had made me look the biggest muppet on God's earth – what a big-shot, infiltrating a small community for five months. For the next two hours, Joe Pestoni held his audience in his hand. You could hear a pin drop. The man was a natural lecturer and presented himself remarkably. Completing his talk he received a standing ovation, of which I am proud to say I was part.

We then retired again to the coffee room where I approached Joe and shook his hand. We both laughed and I was aware that Joe knew exactly how I felt. What an arse I was. Later that evening, along with Ben, Joe and I enjoyed exchanging stories. He was of the opinion that he could not have undertaken undercover work without the comfort of a firearm. Strange to think what we take for granted. It was second nature for us to go into the bad guy's territory unarmed.

We spent the rest of the evening enjoying a 12-year-old malt and learning about each other's lives. Joe had subsequently retired from the FBI and was enjoying life. I would have to say that meeting Joe was the highlight of my career as an undercover police officer. We got on famously and exchanged telephone numbers. Many months later I received an unexpected call from Joe informing me that one of his ex-FBI colleagues – who continues to work deep undercover – was coming to Britain with his wife for a short holiday. Joe said that his friend intended travelling to Scotland and asked me to look after him for a few days. I took this as a great honour and gladly undertook the role of host.

It was now May and my situation and health had not improved. In the middle of May I was summoned to the Deputy Commander's office. He asked me about my welfare. It was at this juncture that I informed him that I had been seeing my own doctor for help. This came as a great surprise to the deputy who enquired as to the reason. I then explained that I had been looking for assistance from the department for some months and it had not been forthcoming, therefore I had taken the matter into my own hands and had attended my doctor voluntarily. This obviously caused the boss some concern. The following morning I received a letter from the force Chief Medical Officer (CMO), inviting me for an interview. On receipt of the letter I approached the Deputy Commander and asked for an explanation. I think the only term I could use would be 'his bottle crashed' and he was covering his own arse.

I duly attended the CMO the following week and there related my story. He was astounded. Unaware that such work was carried out he assured me of his utmost assistance and promise of making further inquiries into psychological support, not only for myself but for other future undercovers. As a result of this interview an appointment was made for me, via the Chief Medical Officer's department, to see a force psychologist some two weeks later. During the interim weeks I continued attending and educating the psychologist on the aspects of police undercover work.

Continuing with my duties became impossible and I needed a break. Once again I went to see my own GP who advised me to report sick. I knew in my own mind that as soon as I called in sick that my ostracism from the undercover network, if not from the crime squad, would be complete. I discussed the matter with Wendy who had been a nurse before joining the police. She knew I was on the edge of a nervous breakdown and had seen the signs for many months. With her support I decided it was now time to lie down and go off sick. Making the decision to fight my illness was in itself a weight off my shoulders.

On the Sunday evening prior to phoning the squad and going off sick I went out on a major binge. The following morning Wendy left me lying in a drunken stupor, sleeping on the settee. I slept until midday, when I awoke to find numerous messages left on the house answering machine from the Detective Sergeant at the squad. After showering and shaving I contacted the force welfare officer and informed her of the circumstances surrounding my absence. I requested that she contact the crime squad and inform them I was now officially reporting sick and requested that nobody from the crime squad contact me until further notice. I had now become bitter about senior management and their lack of support and care.

Later that day I received a telephone call from the same welfare officer informing me that she had contacted the Deputy Commander and that he had been made aware that no members of the management team were to contact me, as per my request. I continued to attend the force psychologist over a period of six months and during such time I reduced my alcohol intake and began to lose some of the 2.5 stones in weight I had gained during Operation Claymore and the subsequent months. I reported sick in mid-July 1997 and was pensioned out in early March 1998.

By November that year most of the court cases surrounding Operation Claymore had been dealt with and only a few remained who had decided to go to trial. During my eight-month absence I received no communication from any of the senior management as I had requested. However, this request was turned around by them and they instructed all my colleagues that absolutely no one was to make contact with me. I read between the lines: the management had panicked, thinking I would have been a disruptive member of the squad and would contaminate my colleagues by telling them the truth as to why I went off sick. Yet again I was being slighted through no fault of my own.

In November that same year I was subject to their final demoralising blow which shouldn't have surprised me. I was punished for going sick, for rocking the boat.

Throughout my 20-odd years in the police service I had numerous appraisals during which time the senior supervisor conducting would ask which areas of the force I did not wish to work within. On every occasion during these years I intimated that I did not wish to work in the division I resided in, for obvious reasons. During my absence, Strathclyde, in unison with the crime squad, decided that it was time for me to rotate and return to division. This was bad enough, however neither the crime squad nor Strathclyde Police 'personnel' department paid heed to my years of requests and duly transferred me to the division I resided in. This news was broken to me via Wendy who, on reading the force bulletin, had noticed my name in the transfer list. This slight set me back yet again and caused me undue stress. The human resources department within Strathclyde Police were evidently not the caring people they purported to be. Obviously no one had looked at my personnel file, or perhaps I am being naive.

Christmas came and went with no contact from the crime squad or Strathclyde. In January I attended a pre-arranged appointment with the Chief Medical Officer. It was at this time that I was informed that, given the circumstances laid before them, the Welfare Department, headed by the CMO, intended to recommend that I should be medically discharged from the police service. No discussion but a finality that came as a severe blow.

For the first time in my life I uttered the words, 'The job's fucked.' Where were the good guys and gaffers when I needed their support? In March that year I was pensioned off from Strathclyde Police through no fault of my own.

Prior to my pension date I contacted the Strathclyde Police Federation and informed them of the full circumstances surrounding my unexpected retirement. They were particularly supportive and suggested with their backing that I undertake a civil action against Strathclyde Police in respect of the neglect of my welfare during my undercover work.

It took almost four years for the case to be given a trial date. It was scheduled for early March 2002. During that four-year period my life slowly returned to normal as did my personality. Approximately ten days prior to the trial, my solicitors and the Strathclyde Police solicitors agreed an amicable financial settlement out of court.

This had been the longest operation I had undertaken and this time there was a successful outcome for both me and my family.

EXTRACTS FROM THE *EVENING CHRONICLE* AND *THE JOURNAL*

A Crown Court judge has formally praised police and civilian workers who took part in a massive Operation Claymore to trap drugs dealers in the Blyth area. The operation was first launched in early in 1996 and has now led to the conviction of more than 20 dealers. On the day of the final defendants being dealt with, Judge Helen Paling sat in a separate court room to commend the undercover detectives who put their lives at risk when they infiltrated south east Northumberland's world of drugs. It has already been revealed that one of the undercover officers had been forced to leave his job because of the stress the job had inflicted on him. There had been 17 drugs-related deaths during the past two years and the dealers arrested have been jailed for a total of 51 years.

Newcastle Crown Court heard 49-year-old John Campbell 'went crackers' during the search at his home in Blyth. He barricaded himself in his bedroom and then lashed out at police who had to break down the door and use CS-gas to subdue him. Campbell was sentenced for two years for charges of supplying drugs and a further two years for assaulting police as they executed a search warrant at his home in Blyth.

A detective who played a key role in the major operation to clean the heroin capital of the north has been pensioned out of the force because of stress. The officer was part of an undercover team planted in Blyth where 17 young people have died of drugs-related deaths in recent years. The investigation, code named Operation Claymore, led to the conviction of more than 20 drugs dealers who have received jail terms totalling more than 51 years.